The BLESSING

GIVING THE GIFT *of* UNCONDITIONAL LOVE AND ACCEPTANCE

John Trent, PhD and Gary Smalley

THOMAS NELSON
Since 1798

NASHVILLE DALLAS MEXICO CITY RIO DE JANEIRO

Published in Nashville, Tennessee, by Thomas Nelson. Thomas Nelson is a registered trademark of Thomas Nelson, Inc.

Thomas Nelson, Inc., titles may be purchased in bulk for educational, business, fund-raising, or sales promotional use. For information, please e-mail SpecialMarkets@ThomasNelson.com.

Unless otherwise noted, all Scripture quotations are taken from the New King James Version®. © 1982 by Thomas Nelson, Inc. Used by permission. All rights reserved.

Scripture quotations noted kjv are from the King James Version.

Scripture quotations noted nasb are taken from the New American Standard Bible®, © The Lockman Foundation 1960, 1962, 1963, 1968, 1971, 1972, 1973, 1975, 1977. Used by permission.

Scripture quotation attributed to the "J. B. Phillips translation" is from *J. B. Phillips: The New Testament in Modern English*, Revised Edition. © J. B. Phillips 1958, 1960, 1972. Used by permission of Macmillan Publishing Co., Inc.

Names have been changed to protect the identities of people referred to in this book.

Library of Congress Cataloging-in-Publication Data

Trent, John, 1952–
    The blessing : giving the gift of unconditional love and acceptance / John Trent and Gary Smalley. — Rev. and updated by John Trent.
       p. cm.
    Includes bibliographical references (p. 259–62).
    ISBN 978-0-8499-4637-0 (trade paper)
    1. Families—Religious life. 2. Child rearing—Religious aspects—Christianity. 3. Blessing and cursing. I. Smalley, Gary. II. Title.
BV4526.3.T74 2011
248.8'45—dc22   2011004971

Printed in the United States of America

11 12 13 14 15 RRD 5 4 3 2 1

To Cindy Trent and Norma Smalley,
who are blessings from God

Contents

CONTENTS

Acknowledgments

My DEEPEST GRATITUDE goes out to my lifelong friend, Gary Smalley, who not only coauthored the original *Blessing* book with me, but who graciously agreed to be the honorary chairman of our National Board of Reference for the Institute for the Blessing. I deeply appreciate his support and that of his outstanding sons and colleagues, Dr. Greg Smalley and Dr. Michael Smalley, at the Smalley Relationship Center.

Thanks also to nine people who have truly been champions in encouraging a new generation of parents to embrace and live out the message of the blessing: Debbie Wickwire, Larry Weeden, Bob Dubberly, Lee Hough, Dewey Wilson, Pastor Ryan Rush, Dr. Royce Fraizer, Dr. Adrian Halverstadt, and Dr. Tony Wheeler. All have been incredible friends and champions for the blessing and the Blessing Challenge. A very special note of thanks to Anne Christian Buchanan. Her extraordinary skill in helping with all the editorial changes and countless wise suggestions on updating the book were absolutely invaluable and deeply appreciated.

The many parents who will see their children's lives changed as they live out the blessing won't know the incredible contribution these ten have made in launching this mission and message, but I'll never forget. Thank you and may God's blessing be on each of you!

ONE

To Change a Life

THE WRITING OF every book has its own story. For me, the story of this book is one that changed my life.

It has now been more than thirty years since two intensely personal experiences collided on the same day. It began on my first day as an intern at a psychiatric hospital. It ended with the Lord opening my eyes to the life-changing power of a simple relational tool called the blessing.

That day at the hospital, I spent a full shift sitting next to a young man on twenty-four-hour suicide watch. He was tall, handsome, well mannered, and an excellent student. In fact, he had been a straight-A student in high school and for three years of college. When he caught the flu the first semester of his senior year, that all changed. In a required PE course he had put off until then, he missed so many classes that his instructor gave him an automatic grade reduction to B for the semester. When the young man found out that there was no extra credit, no way to substitute other classes, and now no way to change his grade or drop the course, he fell into instant despair. He left the teacher's office, went back to his dorm room, and tried to take his life. He would have succeeded had his roommate not unexpectedly and providentially returned.

As we sat and talked, and as I tried not to stare at his bandaged wrists, this young man poured out his heart to me. His story included a brilliant, demanding, engineer father who had gotten straight As himself and demanded nothing less from his oldest son. It highlighted how hard he had tried, all his life, to gain his father's favor. And it ultimately led to how his failing to get an A in a *tennis* class brought the death of a dream—and nearly his own death as well.

This young man desperately yearned for something he couldn't quite define—something that was always in sight, yet somehow never within reach. His heartbreaking tale left a haunting, indelible impression on me. I went home late that afternoon and shared the events of the day at length with my wife, Cindy. While I was still pondering and processing what had happened, the second of two dramatic events took place.

It was nighttime when I finally sat down and began working on a message for a couples' Sunday school class. While I'm sure you would never do such a thing if you were the teacher, I was just beginning my message—for the next day—and kicking myself for letting school, work, and family crowd in so much. Looking back, I can see how Almighty God had his hand in the timing: after sitting down for hours next to that hurting young man, I now sat down and opened my Bible to Genesis 27.

Genesis 27 tells the story of twins: Jacob and Esau. I had read of the struggle between these two brothers countless times in the past. My plan was to speed-read through the passage and throw together a few *inspired* thoughts. Yet that night, with each word I read, time seemed to slow down. It was as if I saw, for the first time, the intensely personal story of how these two young men struggled so mightily to receive the same gift.

In fact, that night, it wasn't just words that I saw. It was like I could see each boy's face. The ear-to-ear smile and unbridled joy in Jacob's eyes when he walked away with his father's blessing. The crushing look of shock and loss on Esau's tormented face when he realized he would never receive that gift.

When Esau lifted up his voice and cried in anguish, "Bless me—me also, O my father!" I suddenly saw not only Esau's unfulfilled longing and broken heart but also an echo of the tears and desperate cries I had heard as I sat next to the heartbroken young man in the hospital. And at that moment, it was as if the Lord put tangible words to the intangible *something* that young man had longed for all his life.

He missed his father's blessing . . . That's what broke his heart!

As that thought washed over me, I read Esau's pitiful, heartbreaking, repeated cry, "Have you only one blessing, my father? Bless me—me also, O my father!" (Gen. 27:38). Just as suddenly, I had words for my own pain and hurt. For all my life I, too, had longed for something I had never received from my own father—his blessing.

Long into the night, I studied and thought and remembered and prayed, and the next day was the first time I taught a group about the blessing. In a small basement classroom at Northwest Bible Church in Dallas, Texas, on a rainy Sunday morning, twenty couples heard about Jacob's gain and Esau's loss. They were the first people I ever asked whether they had received this life-changing gift from their parents.

The impact was incredible. The nodding heads. The tears in too many eyes. The discussion in the hallway, long after class. The calls that came for days afterward from people who felt as if Esau's cry was their own—and from just as many who wanted to make sure they were giving the blessing to their children.

"Can you tell me more about that blessing?"

So began a personal, now thirty-plus-year study of the blessing. It became the subject of my doctoral dissertation and the basis for this book. (The original edition was written with the incomparable Dr. Gary Smalley, who continues to support our blessing ministry in many practical ways.) It also launched seminars and talks I've done and continue to do on the blessing at churches and even stadiums across the country. Rather than adding layers of dust to a stale concept, years of teaching about this amazing Old Testament concept has caused interest to mushroom, not diminish.

When this book was first published, the Internet was reserved for high-end computer users in major universities. Today, blessing messages go out as tweets and e-mails or text messages sent from BlackBerries and iPhones. Yet with all the advances in technology, the challenges of raising children in a world haunted by terrorism and social upheaval has drawn people—more than ever—to want strong, loving families. In that search they keep coming back to God's Word . . . and to the blessing.

Perhaps you are reading this book as a third-generation Christian and have personally benefited from a long tradition of blessing children. If that is the case, you may well find yourself saying, "So *that's* why our family has stayed so close all these years!" Or perhaps you are like my wife, Cindy, and me: first-generation Christians from difficult backgrounds—hers an alcoholic home, mine a single-parent home—each wanting to pass on to our children more than we received. This book can put into words what you missed as a child as well as provide practical, hands-on ways of communicating unconditional love and acceptance to your children and loved ones.

Hardly a day goes by that I don't get an e-mail (and, yes, "snail mail" too) from a joyful, now-grown child whose aging parent finally gave him the blessing for the first time—or from a child who went out of her way to return the blessing to her father or mother and changed their relationship for the better. I hear from athletes and students who never received the blessing at home but who found those life-changing actions and words modeled by a coach, teacher, or youth leader. And I get to read or hear about the excitement and commitment of new fathers and mothers determined to give their newborn child a gift they missed themselves.

Which leads us to today, to this very special edition of *The Blessing*—an ancient, relational, biblical tool whose time has come.

A CALL TO ACTION

Every so often, there comes a unique time, opportunity, or experience. I believe all three happened when you picked up this book.

Today is indeed a unique *time* for you to take part in a significant challenge that launches with this book.

Along the way, you will learn about an unparalleled *opportunity* to create a radically positive *experience* that can be nothing short of life changing for you and for a child in your life.

This new edition of *The Blessing* trumpets a call to action for a huge gathering of parents—literally one million of them—from every corner of our country and world. Men and women who know it's time to go *counterculture* and do something truly great in this age of just getting along.[1]

What is that something great?

Changing the life of just one child.

And how will it get done?

You guessed it—through the blessing.

A powerful relational tool, whose elements were first shared in the Bible, *The Blessing* continues to be reconfirmed in both ongoing and completed clinical studies, providing a model for a strong, thriving family. It's a way of helping children (and adults) experience at the deepest level of their hearts the *certainty* that they are highly valued and forever treasured by someone incredibly significant in their life stories. And it lays out a simple path to follow—five specific actions parents or other caring persons can take, no matter how busy their lives or challenging their circumstances.[2]

The Blessing is not just for children, of course. As we'll see, the principles in this book can transform marriages, friendships, and adult-sibling relationships. Grown children—even those whose parents refused to accept and affirm them—have used these principles to reach out to those very parents in blessing. But because childhood experiences are so powerful in shaping lives, the primary focus of this book is helping adults, especially parents, to give the blessing to children or, as we have said, to just one child.

We all have heard (and by now have mostly grown numb to) television commercials that tug on our heartstrings and implore us to "help the children"—meaning poor kids out there in a different part of town or another country. That's a valuable message, but it is *not* the message of this book. Instead it's about reaching out to that *one child* within your reach and letting your blessing become an agent of life for him or her.

Before we get specific about how the blessing works and how you can give it, let me share with you four reasons why taking the blessing challenge can be so absolutely transformational.

THE BLESSING . . . FIGHTS BACK AGAINST A TOXIC CULTURE

What we are asking you to do in this book runs counter to our dominant culture in these crazy times. With adults working so hard to make ends meet—and some simply preoccupied with their own agendas—there seems to be less and less time for children, and children suffer as a result.

Many children struggle today with what experts call *attachment disorder*. That's the failure of children and young adults to create significant bonds with their parents or others as they get older. They stumble down a road toward broken relationships. They enter young adulthood—and later marriage—with a deep desire for connection but without the understanding, modeling, experience, or confidence that they really *can* build loving, lasting relationships for themselves. They step back from what they want most because they've never seen what it looks like to have someone step toward them.

These are kids who need to experience the blessing in loving homes right now.

Can the blessing challenge reverse this trend?

My experience tells me it can make a big difference—by offering you a strategy for redeeming some of your precious time with your children and strengthening your bond with them. The blessing provides a parenting path that is so practical, so clear, so gently sloped, that if you will just start it, you will soon find yourself gaining momentum in terms of capturing closeness and caring with your family. It offers a way of reclaiming connection with your child no matter how many hours our culture (or your boss) tries to carve out of your month!

THE BLESSING . . . CAN OPEN A CHILD'S HEART TO A LASTING FAITH

According to a recent survey, fully eight out of ten parents report that passing a strong faith to their children was "important" or "very important" to them. Yet while a majority of Americans want these benefits to be a part of their children's lives and futures, studies also show that it's not happening. Depending on which study you choose, anywhere from 40 to 70 percent of children who sit in a second-grade Sunday school class at church today won't be attending any religious services or meetings when they reach their high-school years. In fact, they won't be claiming any kind of growing faith at all.[3]

To understand why this is, it's crucial to understand how a living faith in Christ is successfully transferred. It doesn't happen by teaching a set of rules or customs or passing along a set of traditions, though many think of religion this way. Christianity is and has been primarily about a *relationship*. And the blessing is all about building relationships. When we give children the blessing, we are laying an incredible relational foundation that not only helps them connect with other people but can also prepare their hearts for a relationship with Jesus.

The Blessing Challenge

Calling one million parents to choose to change the life of one child by giving them their blessing. And equipping one thousand churches to create an ongoing culture inside their church that helps parents live out the blessing for a lifetime.

Those are two crucial benefits of taking the blessing challenge. You'll have a tool—no matter how busy you are—to help you battle the cultural phenomenon of attachment disorder with genuine connection. And in learning to give the blessing, you will also be opening a child's heart to a living, lasting faith. But there's also a third benefit.

THE BLESSING . . . CAN HELP HEAL THE HURTS FROM THE PAST

Let's face it. Even those who grow up in the best and most loving of homes can come away with a degree of hurt or disappointment. So how do we cope? Even more important, what can we do to move past the significant damage that a difficult childhood can cause? How can we prevent a painful past from having a negative impact on our present and future relationships? The blessing can make a surprising difference by offering an alternative to damaging self-protective mechanisms we may have developed over the years.[4]

Children simply don't have the maturity or understanding to deal with hurt and pain, so they tend to grab on to anything they can find to protect themselves and help them cope. Whatever works—athletic prowess, academic success, good looks, even drugs or alcohol—they want to repeat. By the time they grow up, they may have created layer upon layer of self-protection.

The trouble is, *self-protection has a shelf life!* Success is fleeting. Looks fade. Addictive substances and activities can bring dramatic life-long damage. More important, none of these self-protective mechanisms offer real, unshakable, lasting confidence and connection—which is exactly what the blessing offers.

Instead of having to wrap themselves in self-protection, children who receive the blessing can be freed to pursue God's best in every area of their lives. And adults can too! My colleague Tony Wheeler and I have seen this again and again in our workshops. As grownups learn to give the blessing to their children, they also learn how to move away from their own hurtful, self-protective pasts.

Imagine not having to live in fear of wrinkles or slowing down. Imagine not having to worry about acquiring all the "toys" someone else has. Imagine moving beyond issues that have held you back for years and finally making peace with your past. That's another life-changing part of experiencing the blessing from God and others—and a third great benefit of taking the blessing challenge.

Here, then, is one last benefit . . .

THE BLESSING . . . IS PART OF YOUR CALL TO A REAL AND RADICAL FAITH

A number of Christian books and messages today call young (and old) believers to a "sold out" life of faith. For example, in reading books such as *Crazy Love* and *Radical*, you find a much-needed call to pursue a Great Commission lifestyle as a real-life goal. But adopting a Great Commission or "missional" lifestyle doesn't mean leaving your important relationships in the dust as you seek to win others for Christ. In fact, if you are not living out a crazy, radical faith and love for Christ with your family and own children first, you have missed a huge first step!

Neglecting to give your own child the blessing because you are too busy with a "higher calling" is to miss the whole point of the gospel. And don't just take that from me. The apostle Paul, who knew a little bit about leading a sold-out life, made it clear that "if anyone does not provide for his own, and especially for those of his household, he has denied the faith and is worse than an unbeliever" (1 Tim. 5:8 NASB).

Building strong relational ties is *part* of your call to radical, sold-out Christianity, and the blessing can be one of your most important tools in ministering to your family and to others. In the process, you will give them the confidence and faith to live their own radical, sold-out lives.

ARE YOU READY TO TAKE THE CHALLENGE?

So enough with all the benefits of giving and living the blessing. It's time to start. Here is a road map for what you will find in each section of the book:

- *Part 1* shares with you just how important the gift of the blessing can be to children—both today and in preparing for their futures.
- *Part 2* shines light on the clear, simple path the Lord has laid out for a parent (or another caring adult)

to follow in giving and living the blessing. It outlines five specific, proven elements that make up the blessing and shows how you can provide each element. Part 2 also challenges you to consider whether you received the blessing as a child and whether you are giving it to your child right now.

- *Part 3* takes an honest look at homes that withhold the blessing and the often emotionally and spiritually devastating consequences that result. You will get an eye-opening picture of why we must choose "life over death, blessing over curse" for each child. But you will also discover how Almighty God provides a way of escape from even the most broken and hurtful past.

- *Part 4* is all about the practicalities of taking the blessing challenge. After understanding what the blessing is and how it can pour hope, life, clarity, and love into a person's life, it's time to take that first step down the blessing path. In this section you will be coached on how to begin writing out a blessing for your child, then sitting down with him or her to share your words in what can be an unforgettable experience for both of you. You will also find encouragement and examples to support you as you continue a life of blessing.

SPECIAL FEATURES OF THIS NEW EDITION

In this revised and updated edition of *The Blessing*, we have built in some additional things to equip and inspire you.

- *Living the Blessing.* Throughout the book you will have the opportunity to stop reading and respond through questions, exercises, and quick ideas for applying the blessing to your life. We encourage you to take advantage of these hands-on opportunities.

- *BlessingLinks.* To further encourage and equip you, you will find strategically placed Internet addresses to sites that will connect you to a wealth of additional resources. Some links will take you to a short free video segment that will follow up on what you've just read, offering additional encouragement and ideas. Other BlessingLinks will connect you with the community of people and the resources on our website, TheBlessing.com, which is rich with stories, tools, courses, and encouragement. Watch for the BlessingLinks icon:

- *The Blessing Challenge.* This book contains everything you need to get started giving the blessing to someone you love. But I hope you consider taking part in the larger effort being launched along with this new edition of *The Blessing.* It's a national initiative called the Blessing Challenge—with a capital *B* and a capital *C.* We are calling one million parents nationwide to take the first step on the blessing path by writing out a blessing and sharing it with a child. And we are challenging and equipping one thousand churches to create an ongoing culture that helps parents live out the blessing for a lifetime. I explain more about this initiative later in the book. I hope you will give some thought to joining the one million parents in a thousand churches who are taking the Blessing Challenge.

Whether or not you choose to join up with the official Blessing Challenge, please be aware that an incredible number of friends and ministries are praying for you and working incredibly hard to do all they can to help you take your first—and second—step down the blessing path. We ask God's most special blessing on you and your family as you read this book and accept the challenge to change lives for the better.

 Congratulations on finishing chapter 1. Please go to TheBlessing. com/Chapter 1 and watch a special video message from Dr. Trent as you start your journey.

PART 1

Why Is the Blessing So Important?

TWO

The Lifelong Search
for the Blessing

ALL OF US long to be accepted by others. While we may say out loud, "I don't care what other people think about me," on the inside we all yearn for intimacy and affection. This yearning is especially true in our relationships with our parents. Gaining or missing out on parental approval has a tremendous effect on us, even if it has been years since we have had any contact with them. In fact, what happens in our relationship with our parents can greatly affect all our present and future relationships. While this may sound like an exaggeration, our offices have been filled with people struggling with this very issue, people just like Brian and Nancy.

THE CRUSHING OF BRIAN'S DREAM

"Please say that you love me, *please!*" Brian's words trailed off into tears as he leaned over the now-still form of his father.

It was late at night in a large metropolitan hospital. Only the cold, white walls and the humming of a heart monitor kept Brian company. His tears revealed a deep inner pain and sensitivity that had tormented him for years. The emotional wounds now seemed beyond repair.

Brian had flown nearly halfway across the country to be at his father's side in one last attempt to reconcile years of misunderstanding and resentment. All his life, Brian had been searching for his father's acceptance and approval, but they always seemed just out of reach.

Brian's father, a career marine officer, wanted nothing more than for his son to follow in his footsteps. With that in mind, he took every opportunity to instill in Brian the discipline and the backbone he would need as a marine.

Words of affection or tenderness were forbidden in their home. It was almost as if Brian's father thought a display of warmth might crack the tough exterior he was trying to create in his son. He drove Brian to participate in sports and to take elective classes that would best equip him to be an officer. But Brian's only praise for scoring a touchdown or doing well in a class was a lecture on how he could and should have done even better.

After graduating from high school, Brian did enlist in the Marine Corps. It was the happiest day of his father's life. However, the joy was short-lived. Cited for attitude problems and disrespect for orders, Brian was soon on report. After weeks of such reports (one for a vicious fight with his drill instructor), Brian was dishonorably discharged from the service as incorrigible.

The news of Brian's dismissal from the marines dealt a deathblow to his relationship with his father. Brian was no longer welcome in his father's home, and for years there was no contact between them.

During those years, Brian struggled with feelings of inferiority and lacked self-confidence. Even though he was above average in intelligence, he worked at various jobs far below his abilities. Three times he got engaged—only to break the engagements just weeks before the weddings. He just couldn't believe another person could really love him.

Brian didn't know that he was experiencing common symptoms of growing up without the family blessing. He knew something was wrong, though, and that sense of something missing finally led him to seek professional help.

I began counseling with Brian after he had broken his third engagement. As he peeled away the layers of his past, Brian began to see both his need for his family's blessing and his responsibility for dealing honestly with his parents. That is when the call came from his mother. His father was dying from a heart attack.

Brian flew immediately to his hometown to see his father. During the entire journey he was filled with hope that now, at long last, they could talk and reconcile their relationship. "I'm sure he'll listen to me. I've learned *so* much. I know things are going to change between us." Brian repeated these phrases over and over to himself as he sat on the plane.

But it was not to be.

Brian's father slipped into a coma a few hours before Brian made it to the hospital. The words that Brian longed to hear for the first time—words of love and acceptance—would never be spoken. Four hours after Brian arrived, his father died without regaining consciousness.

"Dad, please wake up!" Brian's heartbreaking sobs echoed down the hospital corridor. His cries spoke of an incredible sense of loss—not only the physical loss of his father but also the emotional sense of losing any chance of his father's blessing.

NANCY RELIVES A PAINFUL PAST

Nancy's loss was a different sort, but the hurt and pain she received from missing out on the blessing stung her just as deeply and caused problems not only with her parents but with her husband and children as well.

Nancy grew up in an affluent suburb outside a major city. Her mother loved to socialize with other women at the club and at frequent civic activities. In fact, with a marriage that was less than fulfilling, Nancy's mother placed paramount importance on these social gatherings.

When Nancy was very young, her mother would dress her up in elegant clothes (the kind you had to sit still in, not play in) and take her and her older sister to the club. But as Nancy grew older, this practice began to change.

Unlike her mother and older sister, Nancy was not petite. In fact, she was quite sturdy and big boned. Nor was Nancy a model of tranquility. She was a tomboy who loved outdoor games, swinging on fences, and animals of all kinds.

As you might imagine, such behavior from a daughter who was being groomed to be a debutante caused real problems. Nancy's mother tried desperately to mend her daughter's erring ways. Nancy was constantly scolded for being "awkward" and "clumsy." During shopping sprees, she was often subject to verbal barbs designed to motivate her to lose weight.

"All the really nice clothes are two sizes too small for you. They're your *sister's* size," her mother would taunt. Nancy was finally put on a strict diet to try to make her physically presentable to others.

Nancy tried hard to stick to her diet and be all her mother wanted. However, more and more often, Nancy's mother and sister would go to social events and leave Nancy at home. Soon all invitations to join these functions stopped. "After all," her mother told her, "you don't want to be embarrassed in front of all the other children because of the way you look, do you?"

When Nancy first came in for counseling, she was in her thirties, married, and the mother of two children. For years she had struggled with her weight and with feelings of inferiority. Her marriage had been a constant struggle as well.

Nancy's husband loved her and was deeply committed to her, but her inability to feel acceptable left her constantly insecure and defensive. As a result of this hypersensitivity, Nancy felt threatened every time she and her husband began to draw close. Invariably, some small thing her husband did would set her off, and her marriage was back at arm's length.

Frankly, because of her lack of acceptance in the past, being at arm's length was the only place Nancy felt comfortable in any relationship. Her marriage was certainly of concern to her. Yet where Nancy struggled most was with her children, one in particular.

Nancy had two daughters. The older girl was big boned and looked very much like Nancy, but the younger daughter was a beautiful, petite child. What was causing Nancy incredible pain were the relationships between her mother and her children. For once again, her mother catered to the "pretty" daughter while Nancy's older daughter was left out and ignored. Old wounds that Nancy thought were hidden in her past were now being relived through watching her own children. The heartache and loneliness her older daughter was feeling echoed Nancy's unhappiness.

In spite of herself, Nancy found her attitude toward her smaller, daintier daughter changing. The slightest misbehavior from this child would bring an explosion of anger. Bitterness and resentment began to replace genuine affection.

In her heart of hearts, Nancy was also angry at God. In spite of her prayers, she felt he had changed neither her relationship with her mother nor her present circumstances. She felt doomed to repeat her own painful past through her daughters. As a result of this barrage of feelings, she stopped going to Bible study, calling Christian friends, and even praying to God.

Nancy's relationship with her husband, her children, and God had all been affected by missing out on the blessing that she had tried for years to grasp but had never quite been able to reach.

LIVING THE BLESSING

Your Search for the Blessing

Does anything feel familiar to you about Brian's and Nancy's stories? Have you experienced something similar in your life or the life of someone you care about? In what specific ways do you think this situation influences your life today? Write down your thoughts before proceeding to the next chapter.

OUR NEED FOR ACCEPTANCE

For Brian and for Nancy, the absence of parental acceptance held serious consequences. In Brian's case, it kept him from getting close enough to another person to become genuinely committed. In Nancy's, the inability to feel acceptable as a person was destroying her most important relationships. Without realizing it, Brian and Nancy were searching for the same thing—their family's blessing.

Brian and Nancy typify all people who, for one reason

or another, miss out on the blessing. For years after they had moved away from homes *physically*, they still remained chained to the past *emotionally*. Their lack of parental approval in the past kept them from feeling genuinely accepted by others in the present. In Nancy's case, her mother's withheld approval even kept her from believing that her heavenly Father truly accepted her.

Some people are driven toward workaholism as they search for the blessing they never received at home. Always hungry for acceptance and approval, they never feel satisfied that they are measuring up. Others get mired in withdrawal and apathy as they give up hope of ever truly being blessed. Unfortunately, this withdrawal can become so severe that it can lead to chronic depression and even suicide. For almost all children who miss out on their parents' blessing, at some level this lack of acceptance sets off a lifelong search.

The search for the blessing is not just a modern-day phenomenon. It is actually centuries old. In fact, we can find a graphic picture of a person who missed out on his family's blessing in the Old Testament. Let's look now at a confused and angry man named Esau—the one who started my own adventure in learning about the blessing. In so doing we will learn more about the blessing and what it can mean to grow up with or without it.

[THREE]

"Bless Me—Me Also,
O My Father!"

ESAU WAS BESIDE himself. *Could this really be happening?* he may have thought. Perhaps his mind went right back to the events of that day. Just hours before, his father, Isaac, had called him to his side and made a special request. If Esau, the older son, would go and bring in fresh game for a savory meal, Isaac's long-awaited blessing would be given to him.

What was this blessing that Esau had waited for over the years? For sons or daughters in biblical times, receiving their father's blessing was a momentous event. At a specific point in their lives they could expect to feel a loving parent's touch and to hear words of encouragement, love, and acceptance— words that gave them a tremendous sense of being highly valued and that even pictured a special future for them.

We will see that some aspects of this Old Testament blessing were unique to that time. However, the *relationship elements* of this blessing are still applicable today. And although in Old

Testament times the blessing was primarily reserved for only one son and one special occasion, parents today can decide to build these elements of blessing into all their children's lives daily.

Esau's family, of course, had followed their culture's custom of waiting until a specific day to give the firstborn son a blessing, and the long-awaited day had come at last. Esau's time of blessing was supposed to begin as soon as he could catch and prepare the special meal.

With all the skill and abilities of an experienced hunter, Esau had gone about his work quickly and efficiently. In almost no time he had whipped up a delicious stew as only one familiar with the art of cooking in the field could do.

Esau had done just as he was told. Why, then, was Isaac acting so strangely? Esau had just entered his father's tent and greeted him:

> "Let my father arise and eat of his son's game, that your soul may bless me." And his father Isaac said to him, "Who are you?" So he said, "I am your son, your firstborn, Esau."
>
> Then Isaac trembled exceedingly, and said, "Who? Where is the one who hunted game and brought it to me? I ate all of it before you came, and I have blessed him—and indeed he shall be blessed."
>
> When Esau heard the words of his father, he cried with an exceedingly great and bitter cry, and said to his father, *"Bless me—me also, O my father!"* (Gen. 27:31–34, italics added)

Little did Esau know that when his aged and nearly blind father called him to his side, another had been listening. Rebekah, the mother of Esau and his twin brother, Jacob, had also been in the tent. As soon as Esau went out into the fields to hunt fresh game, she had run to her favorite son, Jacob, with a cunning plan.

If they hurried, they could kill a young kid from the flock and prepare a savory meal. What's more, they could dress Jacob in his brother's clothing and put animal skins on him to simulate Esau's rough and hairy arms, hands, and neck.

Putting on Esau's clothes did not present a problem, but one thing they couldn't counterfeit was Esau's voice. That almost blew the whistle on them (v. 22). But even though Isaac was a little skeptical, their plan worked just as they had hoped it would. We read in Genesis 27:22–23, "So Jacob went near to Isaac his father. . . . And he did not recognize him, because his hands were hairy like his brother Esau's hands; so he blessed him." The blessing meant for the older son went to the younger.

Jacob should not have had to trick his way into receiving the blessing. God himself had told Isaac, regarding his twin sons, that the "older shall serve the younger" (Gen. 25:23). Yet Esau had grown up expecting the blessing to be his. No wonder he was devastated when he came back from hunting to find that an even more cunning hunter had stolen into his father's tent and taken what he thought would be his.

Was Esau crying over losing his inheritance? Not really. As we will see later, the oldest son's inheritance was something that came with his birthright and entitled him to a double share in his father's wealth. Yet years before, Esau had already *sold* his birthright to his brother for a pot of red stew (Gen. 25:29–34).

No, Esau wasn't lamenting the fact that he lost the cattle and sheep—he had already despised that gift. What ripped at his heart was something much more personal: his father's blessing. In Old Testament times a father's blessing was irretrievable once it was given, so now Isaac's blessing was forever outside Esau's reach.

Filled with hurt, he cried out a *second* time, "'Do you have only one blessing, my father? Bless me, even me also, O my father.' So Esau lifted his voice and wept" (Gen. 27:38 NASB). In response to his pitiful cries, Esau did receive a blessing of sorts from his father (vv. 39–40), but it was not the words of high value and acceptance that he had longed to hear.

Can you feel the anguish in Esau's cry, "Bless me—me also, O my father"? This same painful cry and unfulfilled longing is being echoed today by many people who are searching for their family's blessing, men and women whose parents, for whatever reason, have failed to bless them with words of love and acceptance. People just like Brian and Nancy. People with whom you rub shoulders every day. Perhaps even you.

THE IMPORTANCE OF THE BLESSING

The hunger for genuine acceptance was a common denominator in Brian's, Nancy's, and Esau's lives—a need that goes unmet in thousands of lives today. The family blessing provides that much-needed sense of personal acceptance. The blessing also plays a part in protecting and even freeing people to develop intimate relationships. Perhaps most important, it lays the foundation for a genuine and fulfilling relationship with God that can survive even the rocky teen years, when many young people pull away from faith.

This is especially important today, in a culture that offers many forms of counterfeit blessing to young people. Cult and gang leaders have mastered the elements of the blessing that we will describe in the pages that follow. Providing a sense of family and offering (at least initially) the promise of personal attention, affection, and affirmation is an important drawing card for many of these groups. And our celebrity-saturated media falsely promises fulfillment and validation through money, fame, sex, and success.

Children who grow up without a sense of parental acceptance are especially susceptible to being drawn in by these counterfeit blessings. In fact, thousands are fooled every year, beckoned like hungry children to an imaginary dinner. But though the aroma of blessing may draw them to the table, after eating they are left hungrier than before.

If you are a parent, learning about the family blessing can help you provide your child(ren) with a protective tool. The best defense against imaginary acceptance is genuine acceptance. By providing genuine acceptance and affirmation at home, you can greatly reduce the likelihood that a child will seek those things in a gang hangout, a cult compound, or an immoral relationship.

Genuine acceptance radiates from the concept of the blessing. However, the blessing is not just an important tool for parents to use. The blessing is also of critical importance for anyone who desires to draw close to another person in an intimate relationship. One of the most familiar verses in the Bible is Genesis 2:24: "For this cause a man shall leave his father and his mother, and shall cleave to his wife" (NASB).

Many books and other resources talk about the need to cleave—or attach firmly—to our spouses. However, very few talk about the tremendous need people also have to "leave" home. Perhaps this is because people have thought of leaving home as simply moving away physically.

In reality leaving home has always meant much more than putting physical distance between our parents and ourselves. In the Old Testament, for example, the farthest most people would actually move away from their parents was across the campfire and into another tent! Leaving home carries with it not only the idea of physical separation but also of *emotional* separation.

The terrible fact is that most people who have missed out on their parents' blessing have great emotional difficulty leaving home in this emotional sense. It may have been years since they have seen their parents, but unmet needs for personal acceptance can keep them emotionally chained to their parents, unable to genuinely cleave to another person in a lasting relationship.

This happened to both Brian and Nancy, and it's an important reason many couples never get off the ground in terms of marital intimacy. You or a loved one may be facing this problem. Understanding the concept of the blessing is crucial to defeating the problem and freeing people to build healthy relationships.

LIVING THE BLESSING

Blessings That Aren't Really Blessings

Make a list of "counterfeit blessings" that have tempted you and other people you know. Which are the most difficult to resist? Do you think all of these are dangerous? If not, what determines the difference between a harmless diversion or pastime and a treacherous counterfeit?

A JOURNEY OF HOPE AND HEALING

In a world awash with insecurity and in search of acceptance, we need biblical anchors to hold on to—anchors like the blessing.

The search for acceptance that Brian and Nancy went

through and so many others undertake often leads people to accept a cure that is worse than the problem itself. (Many addictions, for instance, have their roots in the deep loneliness of growing up without a parent's blessing.) In contrast, God's Word and his principles offer a dependable blueprint for constructing or reconstructing truly healthy relationships.

In the pages that follow, you will discover more about the blessing. You will explore the five crucial elements that make up the blessing—and make it so powerful. You will also have a chance to look back and evaluate whether you received the blessing as a child, how this childhood experience affects you and your family today, and how—if you missed out on the blessing—you can find healing.

Most important, if you are a parent, you will discover how to make sure your children—toddlers to teens, and even those who are grown—receive the blessing from you. In the process, you will be exposed to God's spiritual family blessing that is offered to each of his children.

If you are a teacher, discovering the blessing can help you better understand your students. If you counsel others, it can provide a helpful framework for understanding many problems and offering practical solutions. If you are involved in ministering to others, it can help you understand this crucial need every person has and provide some resources for meeting that need.

Our prayer is, in the following pages, you will take the time and have the courage to journey into the past, a journey that can lead to hope and healing. Even more, we pray that you will be willing to look honestly at the present and apply what you discover.

These pages may end your lifelong search for acceptance or begin a new relationship with your children, your spouse, your parents, or a close friend. Our deepest desire is that this book will enrich your relationship with your heavenly Father as you learn more about the source of blessing that he is to each believer. All this as we take our first look at the life-changing concept called the blessing.

[FOUR]

A Life-and-Death Choice

WHEN I WAS young, my grandparents came to live with us for several years to "help out" with three very rambunctious boys. My grandfather was a wonderful man but a stern disciplinarian. He had rules for everything, with swats to go along with all his rules. And there was one ironclad rule that we hated because it carried two automatic swats: "Be home before the streetlight comes on."

There was no "grading on the curve" in my home. And while spanking may be controversial in many homes, there was no discussion when my grandfather moved in. With the streetlight planted right in our yard, all he had to do was look out the kitchen window and see if we had made it home in time. And one night my twin brother, Jeff, and I didn't.

Never one to delay punishment, I shuffled down the hallway to Grandfather's room and received my two swats. But little did I know that I was moments away from gaining one of the most significant blessings in my life.

After my spanking, my grandmother told me to go back

down the hall and call my grandfather for dinner. I didn't feel much like being polite to him at the time, but I didn't want to risk another spanking either. So off I went to his room.

While many children grow up with open access to their elders' rooms, we didn't. We were to knock on Grandfather's door, ask for permission to enter, and always call him "Grandfather" or "Sir" when we addressed him.

I meant to knock on the door, but then I noticed it was already slightly ajar. That's when I broke the rule and gently pushed it open to look inside.

What I saw shocked me. My grandfather, a man who rarely showed any emotion, was sitting on the end of the bed, crying. I stood at the door in confusion. I had *never* seen him cry, and I didn't know what to do.

Suddenly he looked up and saw me, and I froze where I was. *I hope catching him crying isn't a sixty-swat offense!* I thought to myself.

Yet my grandfather simply said to me, his voice full of emotion, "Come here, John."

When I reached him, he reached out and hugged me closely. Then, in tears, he told me how much he loved me and how deeply it hurt him to have to spank me. "John," he said, seating me on the bed next to him and putting his big arms around me, "I want more than anything in life for you and your brothers to grow up to become godly young men. I hope that you know how much I love you and how proud I am of you."

I can't explain it, but when I left his room that night, I was a different person because of my grandfather's blessing. As I look back today, I see that evening provided me with a meaningful rite of passage from childhood to young adulthood. For years afterward, recalling that clear picture of my grandfather's blessing helped point me toward a more positive future and shape my attitudes and actions.

A few months later my grandfather died instantly and unexpectedly of a cerebral aneurysm. I know now that the Lord allowed me, for that one and only time, to hear and receive the blessing from him. While I would never receive the blessing from my own father, I did receive it that day from my grandfather.

Why the Blessing Matters

Just what is this blessing that seems to be so important? Does it really apply to us today, or was it just for Old Testament times? What are the elements of which it consists? How can I know whether I have received it or if my children are experiencing it now?

These questions commonly surface when I introduce people to the blessing. In answering them, we will discover five powerful relationship elements that the Old Testament blessing contains. The presence or absence of these elements can help us determine whether our home is—or our parents' home was—a place of blessing.

A study of the blessing always begins in the context of parental acceptance. However, in studying the blessing in the Scriptures, we found that its principles can be used in any intimate relationship.

Husbands can apply these principles in blessing their wives, and wives their husbands.

Friendships can be deepened and strengthened by including each element of the blessing.

These key ingredients, when applied in a church family, can bring warmth, healing, and hope to our brothers and sisters in Christ, many who never received an earthly blessing from their parents. As we will see in a later chapter, they are the very relationship elements God uses in blessing his children.

Perhaps the best place to begin our look at the benefits of giving or gaining the blessing is to dig into the biblical ideas behind the *blessing*—and the clear choice inherent in the word.

THE BLESSING AND THE CHOICE

Perhaps one of the clearest ways to begin to understand what the blessing means is to look at an amazing choice God once laid before his people—the same choice that I believe is put in front of each of us today, a choice that is literally a matter of life and death. It's found in an amazing passage in the book of Deuteronomy, in the words that God spoke to Joshua:

> I call heaven and earth to witness against you today, that I have set before you life or death, the blessing and the curse. So choose life in order that you may live, you and your descendants. (Deut. 30:19 NASB)

The context in which these words were spoken can help us understand this idea of a choice. Joshua is the new leader of God's people. They have traveled all the way from Egypt, and right now they are finally ready to take their first steps into the promised land. Almighty God lays before them a path that he wants them to follow—one that begins with a crucial choice or, actually, two choices.

The first choice set before his people: life or death.

The second: blessing or curse.

Let's define our terms so we really understand how important these choices were to the Israelites . . . and how they can affect our relationship with God and others today.

A MATTER OF LIFE AND DEATH

The Hebrew word translated *life* in this passage carries with it the idea of movement.[1] In other words, things that are alive are things that are moving. Specifically, they're moving toward someone or something. So the first choice we have is to move toward God and toward others. When we do that, we add life to our relationships.

Think about a couple you know who have a great marriage. Almost always you will notice that they *take steps* to move toward each other—not just physically but emotionally. They choose to do things together. They choose to walk together toward a goal or interest or area they like.

Choosing life, then, means getting busy in moving toward the Lord or others. But there's the other side of this choice in the Deuteronomy passage as well. We can also choose death.

Interestingly, the word translated *death* also carries with it the concept of movement—in fact, its literal meaning is "to step away."[2] The idea is that death is stepping away from others, from life, from what we have built or shared with others.

Let's go back to our example of the couple. As a marriage counselor, time and again I've seen one spouse (or both) take a *step away* from the other when challenges come up. When they do this, something starts dying in their relationship. The more they move away from each other, the more problematical their marriage becomes.

So that's the life-or-death choice when it comes to relationships. At any given juncture we make the choice to move toward the other person, choosing life in that relationship, or to step away, choosing death.

TO BLESS OR TO CURSE

To understand the second choice set before God's people in Joshua's time and in ours today—the blessing and the curse—let's take another look at the Hebrew words. For they also imply two very different paths we can choose to take with the Lord and with others.

The first idea contained in the Hebrew word for "bless" is that of "bowing the knee."[3] (Genesis 24:11 actually uses this word to describe a camel who must bend its knees so its master can get on.) Bowing before someone is a graphic picture of valuing that person.

Most Americans have never actually seen one person bow before another. But in biblical times (and in many cultures today), you bowed before someone of great value—a king, a queen, a prophet, someone considered important and of high worth. When you bless someone, in other words, you are really saying, "I choose to treat you as someone incredibly valuable in my life." Of course, when we say, "Bless the Lord!" we're saying that as well: "Lord, you are so incredibly valuable, you're worthy of our 'bowing the knee' before you."

Along with this first picture comes a second biblical word picture. The word for *bless* (and a similar word, for *honor*) also carries the idea of adding weight or value to someone.[4] Literally, it's a picture of adding coins to a scale. In biblical times, you didn't just hand someone a coin with a specific denomination stamped on it as we do today. In Old Testament times, a coin might carry an inscription or even a picture of a ruler or someone of great value. But the way you determined how much it was worth was to put it on a scale. The greater the weight, the higher the value.

Let's put those two pictures together now to gain a sharper focus on what it means to bless someone. You are basically saying, "You are of such great value to me, I choose to add to your life." And as you'll soon see, there are five specific actions you can take (the five elements of the blessing) to do just that for another person.

But what about the opposite choice—the curse? In understanding the word picture behind this word, I think you'll see it's a choice that many continue to make today. It's not just a Stephen King scenario, an occult choice that belongs in horror movies. Any of us can make the choice to curse others instead of blessing them. We do that when we subtract the things that would add life for the other person.

The word for *curse* in this passage literally means a "trickle" or "muddy stream" caused by a dam or obstruction upstream.[5] For Joshua's people, living in desert lands, cutting off water meant cutting off life itself. So do you get the terrible word picture here? When we curse someone, we are choosing to "dam up the stream" on life-giving actions and words that could flow down to that person.

Think of a desert dweller in biblical times who walks for miles to find a life-giving stream, only to get there and find a muddy trickle because someone dammed up the stream. But now picture someone choosing to break down the dam—choosing to add what was missing, bringing life where there had been death.

A beautiful example of this is found in John 4, when Jesus sat down with the woman at the well. We look at the story in detail in a later chapter, but let's take a quick peek now. This woman is more or less an outcast in her town—married five times, now living out of wedlock with a sixth man. She comes to draw water in the heat of the day, when no one else is around, probably avoiding the other women in the village. And she's a Samaritan, looked down on by all Jews. So many aspects of her life act to dam up the flow of blessing in her life—by that definition, she's cursed.

But do you remember what Jesus offers this woman? He offers her "living water" (John 4:10–15). And that's because God is the one who can break down all the things in our lives that curse us, slowing the flow of what we need to a trickle. It is he who blesses us with a flow of living water.

In Deuteronomy 23:5, God puts it this way: "The LORD your God would not listen to Balaam [someone hired by the Hebrews' enemies to curse them], but the LORD your God turned the curse into a blessing for you, because the LORD your God loves you."

That's God's choice, of course, but the choice to bless or curse others is ours as well. We are told in the book of Proverbs that "death and life are in the power of the tongue" (Prov. 18:21). So it is with the blessing, and so it is in a terribly negative way when we choose the curse.

It's our choice then—yours and mine.

Will we choose life and move toward others or choose death and step away?

Will we choose to bless our loved ones and the Lord by bowing our knee and weighing our scales in their favor— opening our lives to God's blessing in the process? Or will we choose to curse them by blocking the flow of good things in our own lives and others'?

If you are ready to choose life and blessing, let's be even

more specific about those five elements of the blessing that biblical parents gave and that children today—children of all ages—long for as well.

 For more thoughts on the importance of making that life-or-death choice to bless another person, especially a child, watch the video provided at TheBlessing.com/Chapter 4.

PART 2

Understanding the Blessing

[FIVE]

A Clear Path for Every Parent

THERE ARE TIMES in our lives when being able to see a clear path is crucial. That was certainly true on a rainy August day a number of years ago, when two young adventurers decided to scale Mount Dom, the highest summit wholly within Switzerland. At 14,942 feet, this peak near the town of Zermatt is higher even than the Matterhorn.

Even though these American tourists were young and inexperienced mountaineers, they felt confident that they could make their climb with ease. After all, their first-day goal was only to go halfway up the mountain to the Dom's "high hut," which was staffed that time of year by the Swiss Alpine Club. They would spend the night at the hut, get up early the next morning, and reach the summit with no problem.

At least that was their plan.

Despite a late start and deteriorating weather conditions, they set out enthusiastically, moving up the forested trail toward the halfway house. Because they hadn't planned on being out all night, they hadn't bothered to bring any cold-weather gear. They soon regretted that fact when the clouds started spitting drops and then a steady rain began to fall. What's more, as they climbed higher and crossed the timberline, the temperature fell dramatically.

By six o'clock that evening, when the cold rain began to turn into snow, they were still climbing. They had long since crossed the timberline, and the trail before them had become increasingly difficult to follow. By eight o'clock, darkness had fallen, and they both began to realize they weren't just lost—they were in life-threatening trouble. They were soaked, shivering, and at risk of hypothermia, and darkness was swallowing the path. They had no way of knowing whether they were still headed toward the high hut or headed toward one of the many steep drop-offs that hugged the trail they had been climbing.

Just when their situation was most desperate, something miraculous happened. From a great distance away, a tiny light began to flicker. It just popped up on the mountainside like a star beginning to blaze in the sky. Even at a distance, the glow looked as bright as a lighthouse beacon to those two shivering, frightened young men.

Where did the light come from? Before retiring for the night, the keeper of the Dom's high hut had decided to step outside and place a kerosene lamp next to the door—just in case a beacon might be needed by anyone caught in the worsening storm. That light drew the boys out of the life-threatening cold and darkness and into a place of warmth and safety.

That story provides a context for the importance of a clear path in times of increasing darkness—like these times in which we live. If we are serious about helping our children move toward warmth and light and love, we need to light their footsteps on just such a positive path. The blessing is the best way I know to provide such a light.

The Five Elements of the Blessing

But what exactly does it mean to give a blessing? What actions and attitudes combine to make this biblical tool so uniquely effective?

The blessing as described in Scripture always included five elements:

1. Meaningful and appropriate touch
2. A spoken message
3. Attaching high value to the one being blessed
4. Picturing a special future for him or her
5. An active commitment to fulfill the blessing

Let's take a quick look at each of these before exploring them all in greater depth.

Meaningful Touch

Meaningful touch was an essential element in bestowing the blessing in Old Testament homes. So it was with Isaac when he went to bless his son. We read in Genesis 27:26 that Isaac said, "Come near now and kiss me, my son." This incident was not an isolated one. Each time the blessing was given in the Scriptures, a meaningful touch provided a caring background to the words that would be spoken. Kissing, hugging, or the laying on of hands were all a part of bestowing the blessing.

Meaningful touch has many beneficial effects. As we will see in the next chapter, the act of touch is key in communicating warmth, personal acceptance, affirmation, even physical health. For any person who wishes to bless a child, spouse, or friend, touch is an integral part of that blessing.

A Spoken Message

The second element of the blessing involves a spoken message—one that is actually put into words. In many homes today such words of love and acceptance are seldom received. Parents in these homes assume that simply being present communicates the blessing—a tragic misconception. A blessing fulfills its purpose only when it is actually verbalized—spoken in person, written down, or preferably both.

For a child in search of the blessing, silence communicates mostly confusion. Children who are left to fill in the blanks when it comes to what their parents think about them will often fail the test when it comes to feeling valuable and secure. Spoken or written words at least give the child an indication that he or she is worthy of some attention. I learned this lesson on the football field.

When I began playing football in high school, one particular coach thought I was filled with raw talent (emphasis on *raw*!). He was constantly chewing me out, and he even took extra time after practice to point out mistakes I was making.

After I missed an important block in practice one day (a frequent occurrence), this coach stood one inch from my face mask and chewed me out six ways from Sunday. When he finally finished, he had me go over to the sidelines with the other players who were not a part of the scrimmage.

Standing next to me was a third-string player who rarely got into the game. I can remember leaning over to him and saying, "Boy, I wish he would get off my case."

"Don't say that," my teammate replied. "At least he's talking to you. If he ever *stops* talking to you, that means he's given up on you."

Many adults we see in counseling interpret their parents' silence in exactly that same way. They feel as though they were third-string children to their parents. Their parents may have provided a roof over their heads (or even a Porsche to drive), but without actual words of blessing, they were left unsure of how much they were valued and accepted.

Abraham spoke his blessing to his son Isaac. Isaac spoke a blessing to his son Jacob. Jacob gave a verbal blessing to each of his twelve sons and to two of his grandchildren. When God blessed us with the gift of his Son, it was his *Word* that "became flesh and dwelt among us" (John 1:14). God has always been a God of words.

"But I don't yell at my children or cut them down like some parents," some may say. Unfortunately, the lack of negative words will not necessarily translate into a verbal blessing. We will see this lack illustrated through several painful examples in a later chapter.

To see the blessing bloom and grow in the life of a child, spouse, or friend, we need to verbalize our message. Good intentions aside, good *words*—spoken, written, and preferably both—are necessary to communicate genuine acceptance.

Attaching High Value

Meaningful touch and a spoken (or written) message—these first two elements lead up to the content of the words themselves. To convey the blessing, the words must attach high value to the person being blessed.

In blessing Jacob (thinking it was Esau), Isaac said, "Surely, the smell of my son is like the smell of a field which the Lord has blessed. . . . Let peoples serve you, and nations bow down to you" (Gen. 27:27, 29).

That pictures a very valuable person! Not just anybody merits having nations bow down to him! And while we might think that calling a person a field would be criticizing him, that is not the case. A *blessed* field was one where there was tremendous growth and life and reward. Just ask a farm kid what a record crop, all ready to harvest, means to his or her parents. That's the picture Isaac gives his son.

As you may have noticed, Isaac uses a word picture (the field) to describe how valuable his son is to him. Word pictures are a powerful way of communicating acceptance. Later we will look at the use of these word pictures and learn how to use them in giving a blessing. In the Old Testament they were a key to communicating to a child, spouse, or friend a message of high value—the third element of the family blessing.

Picturing a Special Future

A fourth element of the blessing is the way it pictures a special future for the person being blessed. Isaac said to his son Jacob, "May God give you of the dew of heaven, of the fatness of the earth. . . . Let peoples serve you, and nations bow down to you" (Gen. 27:28–29).

Even today, Jewish homes are noted for picturing a special future for their children. One story I heard illustrates this activity very well.

Sidel, a young Jewish mother, was proudly walking down the street, pushing a stroller with her infant twins. As she rounded the corner, she saw her neighbor, Sarah. "My, what beautiful children," Sarah cooed. "What are their names?" Pointing to each child, Sidel replied, "This is Bennie, the doctor, and Reuben, the lawyer."

This woman believed her children had great potential and a special future before them. Isaac believed the same about his son and communicated that in his blessing—as we should communicate to those we seek to bless.

One distinction should be made between Isaac's blessing and the act of picturing a special future for a person today. Because of Isaac's unique position as a patriarch (God's appointed leader and a father of the nation of Israel), his words to Jacob carried with them the weight of biblical prophecy. We today cannot predict another person's future with such biblical accuracy. But we can help those we are blessing see a future that is full of light and opportunity. We can let them know we believe they can build an outstanding life and future with the strengths and abilities God has given them.

As we will see in a later chapter, our Lord himself speaks quite eloquently about our future in the Bible. In fact, he goes to great lengths to assure us of our present relationship with him and of the ocean full of blessings in store for us as his children.

We need to picture just such a special future for our children if we are serious about giving them our blessing. With this fourth element of the blessing, a child can gain a sense of security in the present and grow in confidence to serve God and others in the future.

An Active Commitment

The last element of the blessing concerns the responsibility that goes with giving the blessing. For the patriarchs, not only their words but God himself stood behind the blessing they bestowed on their children. Several times God spoke directly through the angel of the Lord to the patriarchs confirming his active commitment to their family line.

Parents today, in particular, need to rely on the Lord to

give them the strength and staying power to confirm their children's blessing by expressing such an active commitment. They, too, have God's Word through the Scriptures as a guide, plus the power of the indwelling Holy Spirit.

Why is active commitment so important when it comes to bestowing the blessing? Words alone cannot communicate the blessing; they need to be backed with a willingness to do everything possible to help the one blessed be successful. We can tell a child, "You have the talent to be a very good pianist." But if we neglect to provide a piano for that child to practice on, our lack of commitment has undermined our message.

When it comes to spending time together or helping develop a certain skill, some children hear, "Wait until the weekend." Then it becomes, "Wait until *another* weekend" so many times that they no longer believe the words of blessing.

The fifth element of the blessing, an active commitment, is crucial to communicating the blessing in our homes.

At Home with the Family Blessing

That's a brief overview of the five elements of the blessing that can become a life-changing part of how we *do* family. Provide the five basic ingredients of the blessing—meaningful touch, a spoken (or written) message, attaching high value to the one being blessed, picturing a special future for him or her, and confirming the blessing by an active commitment—and personal acceptance can thrive in a home.

Our aim now is to become very practical as we look more closely at each of the five key elements of the blessing. For each element you will be prompted to look back at the path you walked with your own parents and ask, "Did I receive this element of the blessing?" Then a little later you will be prompted to consider the path you are walking with your child today and to ask, "Am I giving this element of the blessing to my child?" Both questions, as we go through each of these five elements, can provide a powerful, thought-provoking look at where you have been, where you are today, and where you can go as you accept the challenge of making the blessing part of your family life.

If you are a little unclear right now as to why these five elements are so significant, get ready for the light to be turned up brighter on this biblical path . . . starting with our look at each child's need for appropriate, meaningful touch.

SIX

The First Element:
Meaningful Touch

ISABEL WAS A sensitive young woman—and a seriously ill one, suffering greatly in the diabetic/medical-surgical unit. She was in so much pain that she cried regularly to the nursing staff, pleading for more frequent painkiller injections. Yet the medicine therapy she was on and her own physical condition precluded her from receiving the shots when she wanted them. The risk for further infection and internal bleeding was simply too great.

Finally, after Isabel had badgered the nurses on every shift, the senior nurse in charge went to talk to her.

Nurse Ida Heath was a thirty-year veteran of the wards and a reserved, capable teacher. She explained to Isabel, logically and practically, the potential dangers of giving her injections whenever she asked for them. She also assured Isabel that the nurses were trying to protect her, not harm her, by limiting her injections. Isabel listened intently and even nodded, understanding.

Her mission accomplished, Nurse Heath was preparing to leave when Isabel stopped her. "If I can't have my shot . . . *can you give me a hug?*"

Not thinking she had heard right, the nurse asked, "Excuse me?"

Isabel repeated, "Could you give me a hug for the pain . . . *please?*"

Caught off guard, the stately nurse said, "Well, okay," and put an arm around Isabel's shoulder. But then, it was as if God spoke to her and said, "For goodness' sake, Ida, that's not what she asked for!" So Nurse Heath put both arms around Isabel and gave her a big hug.

Isabel burst into tears.

"All this time I thought the nurses hated me. I'm just hurting so badly. Whenever I need a pain shot, can I call you and get a hug instead?"

Nurse Heath assured Isabel she could get her hug whenever she needed it. She even wrote it down on her medical Kardex, in the medication section: "Pain hugs for Isabel, upon request."

Isabel died a few months later at the age of thirty-four. But before her death, whenever she was admitted to a different ward in the hospital or when the nights became too long, she would call Nurse Heath for her pain hug.

A hug can't wipe away all our pain, but it can help. And while meaningful touch can't chase away all our fears and insecurities, it can help with many of them.

A little four-year-old girl became frightened late one night during a thunderstorm. After one particularly loud clap of thunder, she jumped up from her bed, ran down the hall, and burst into her parents' room. Jumping right in the middle of the bed, she sought out her parents' arms for comfort and assurance.

"Don't worry, honey," her father said, trying to calm her fears. "The Lord will protect you." The little girl snuggled closer to her father and said, "I know that, Daddy, but right now I need someone with skin on!"

The honesty of some children! This little one did not doubt her heavenly Father's ability to protect her, but she was also aware that he had given her an earthly father she could run to, someone whom God had entrusted with a special gift that could bring her comfort, security, and personal acceptance—the blessing of meaningful touch.

This little girl was fortunate. Her father was willing to share this important aspect of the blessing with his daughter. Not all children are as fortunate. Even in caring homes, most parents, particularly fathers, will stop touching their children once they reach the grade-school years.[1] When they do that, an important part of their blessing stops as well.

Holding and hugging a four-year-old is permissible in most homes. But what about the need a fourteen-year-old has to be meaningfully touched by his mother or father (even if the teenager outwardly cringes every time she or he is hugged)? What about a thirty-four-year-old—or a spouse or close friend?

We all need meaningful touch and suffer when we are deprived of it. However, children are particularly affected by the absence of touch. Sometimes it can so affect a child that he or she spends a lifetime reaching out for arms that will never embrace him or her.

"I wish . . . I wish . . ." Lisa had slumped down in her chair, hugging herself and rocking back and forth as she repeated these words. Lisa was a new adolescent patient in the psychiatric ward where I was an intern. Whenever she felt afraid or sad, she would wrap her arms around herself and rock back and forth.

We found that Lisa had behaved this way since she was seven years old. That was when her mother abandoned her at an orphanage.

Lisa was trying to escape her hurt and pain by *holding herself.* She had no one else to hold her; all she had was the wish that her mother would return. She needed meaningful touch so much that she would wrap her arms around herself and try to hug away the hurt.

THE BLESSING: MEANINGFUL TOUCH

In the Scriptures, touch played an important part in the bestowal of the family blessing. When Isaac blessed Jacob, an embrace and a kiss were involved. We read, "Then his father Isaac said to him, 'Please come close and kiss me, my son'" (Gen. 27:26 NASB).

The Hebrew word for "come close" is very descriptive. It is used of armies drawn together in battle. It is even used to picture the overlapping scales on a crocodile's skin.[2] It may have been awhile since you last saw a battle or a crocodile, but these word pictures still call up in our minds a picture of a very close connection.

Isaac wasn't asking his son to give him an "Aunt Ethel hug." (Remember Aunt Ethel—the one who pinched your cheek and then repeatedly patted you on the back when she hugged you?) Free from the current taboos our culture sets on a man embracing his son, Isaac was calling Jacob close to give him a bear hug.

For fathers in North America, there is a strong correlation between the age of a son and whether his father will touch him.[3] Yet Isaac's grown son was at least *forty years old* when he said, "Come close and kiss me, my son."[4]

Children of all ages need meaningful touch, particularly from a father. Studies have showed that mothers touch their children in more nurturing ways and fathers in more playful ways. But when the children were interviewed, they perceived their fathers' touch as more nurturing—perhaps because it didn't happen as often.[5]

As we have seen with Lisa, our need for meaningful touch does not go away when we enter grade school. Isaac didn't set up barriers around the need to be touched. He was a model that parents, husbands and wives, and even friends at church need to follow in giving the blessing.

I deeply appreciate my mother's commitment to meaningfully touch us when we were children even though I did not always appreciate it at the time.

As a single parent, Mom had to work full time to support three hungry, healthy boys. In the morning she would get us all up and get herself ready. Then we would all pile in the car so she could take us off to school and herself to work. While her taxi service saved us the long walk, there was one thing about it that my twin brother and I hated. Before we were allowed to get out of the car, we had to give Mom a hug.

As you can imagine, hugging your mom in front of all your school friends was not tops on the list of two aspiring football players. In fact, each year we would make our mother drop us farther and farther from school—just in case someone saw us hugging her. But she never stopped. Her pattern of hugging us was absolutely dependable, even when we would respond with "Oh, Mom!" or "I can't stand it!" I can remember only one time when it didn't happen, and it got me in major trouble.

On that particular morning, we were all in a rush to get the day launched. We were eager to get to school to shoot some hoops before the morning bell, and Mom had a major presentation at work. Distracted by her busy day, she let us all out of the car without forcing us to give her a hug.

As she drove away, Jeff and I just looked at each other. She hadn't even *mentioned* hugging us—and I instantly thought the worst.

"She must know something," I told Jeff. "I *know* she knows something!"

Unfortunately, at the time there were a number of things she could have found out that could have resulted in our being grounded until we were in our midthirties.

All day we brooded over what our mother might have discovered that made her so angry she had chosen not to hug us. Finally the day was over, and we all sat around the dinner table. Dinnertime at our house was normally filled with enthusiastic conversation, but that night there was dead silence as we waited for the storm to break. While Jeff could have waited all night, the quiet quickly got to me. I broke down and blurted out, "Okay, Mom. We're sorry. I can't believe you found out, but we are *really* sorry."

I wasn't ready for the confused look that came across my mother's face.

"What are you talking about, John?" she asked.

"Well, this morning," I told her. "When we got out of the car . . . you know . . . you didn't hug us!"

Laughing, she said, "Oh, I'm sorry. I guess I was so busy thinking about the presentation I had to make, I just forgot." Then her smile vanished. "But what was it you were confessing to?"

As Jeff glared at me, I realized I had just gotten us both in big trouble—all because I had missed the hug I always hated.

Though I could always count on my mother's touch,

the opposite was true of my father. With him, I could rely on touch being off-limits. When my brothers and I finally began a relationship with him after nearly fifteen years of his absence, it was obvious that meaningful touch wasn't something he was comfortable with.

During my easily embarrassed teenage years, that was all right with me. But as the years went on, I found myself wishing for at least one hug from my father. At my wedding. Or when our daughter Kari was born. Or when Laura, our second "gift" and blessing, arrived. Or at Christmastime. Or anytime.

I did hold his hand on a few occasions—when he was so seriously ill he couldn't object. And each of those times stands out like a beacon—a memory of closeness that was pushed away from me anytime he had the strength.

LIVING THE BLESSING

Meaningful Touch and You

As you read about this first element of the blessing, take time to write down some of your thoughts and feelings. In particular, how did you experience this element in your early life? Was meaningful touch an active, positive part of your past? Why or why not? What part did it play in whether or not you received the blessing as a child?

ANOTHER TOUCHING SCENE

In the Scriptures, we find another clear example of including meaningful touch in bestowing the blessing. This time the blessing involves a grandfather who wanted to make sure his grandchildren received this special gift of personal experience. Let's look in on the "touching" scene:

> Joseph said to his father, "They are my sons, whom God has given me in this place." And he said, "Please bring them to me, and I will bless them." Now the eyes of Israel were dim with age, so that he could not see. Then Joseph brought them near him, and he kissed them and embraced them. . . .
>
> Then Israel stretched out his right hand and laid it on Ephraim's head . . . and his left hand on Manasseh's head. (Gen. 48:9–10, 14)

Jacob (whose name had now been changed to Israel) not only kissed his grandchildren and held them close, but he also placed his hands on each grandson's head.[6] This practice of laying on of hands was an important part of many of the religious rituals for the biblical patriarchs.

There are at least two important reasons why placing our hands on someone as a part of the blessing is so special. First, there is a symbolic meaning attached to touching, and second, there are tremendous physical benefits to the laying on of hands.

THE SYMBOLIC MEANING PICTURED BY TOUCHING

In the Old Testament, the symbolic picture of the laying on of hands was important. This touch presented a graphic picture of transferring power or blessing from one person to another.[7]

For example, in the book of Leviticus, Aaron was instructed to use this practice in his priestly duties. On the Day of Atonement, he was to place his hands on the head of a goat that was then sent into the wilderness. This picture is of Aaron symbolically transferring the sins of Israel onto that animal. (It is also a prophetic picture of how Christ, like that spotless animal, would take on our sins at the Cross.) In another example, Elijah passed along his role as God's prophet to Elisha by the laying on of hands.

Even today the symbolic meaning of touch is powerful. While we may not be consciously aware of it, the way we touch can carry tremendous symbolic meaning.

A young woman holding hands with a new boyfriend can signal "I'm taken" to other would-be suitors. Two business-people shaking hands can signify that an important deal has been completed. A minister at a wedding says to a couple, "If you then have freely and lawfully chosen one another as husband and wife, please *join hands* as you repeat these vows."

Back in the 1990s, near the end of the first Gulf War, I witnessed an example of the symbolic meaning of touch at one of my favorite places to watch human behavior—the airport.

A young Japanese American soldier sat next to me on a plane coming from Ontario to Phoenix. He was on his way home from almost six months in the Gulf. I learned he had ridden a tank through the heaviest fighting. He told of firefights at night, burning oil wells, jubilant Kuwaitis who had been defended from Saddam Hussein's attack, and of missing home. Then our plane touched down.

At the Phoenix airport, a glass wall separates the passengers who have been screened from family and friends who have come to meet them. As we rounded the corner, we heard cries of joy.

There, pounding on the glass wall, were the soldier's wife, two sets of parents, and two young children. While Asians are often stereotyped as reserved, there was nothing reserved about this young hero's reception. He ran through the exit doors and into his family's arms to be smothered with hugs, kisses, smiles, and tears. All of us in the waiting area were caught up in this wonderful reunion. Total strangers spontaneously burst into applause, and many had tears in their eyes as we all shared in the happiness of this homecoming.

Just a few months later, I saw a different type of homecoming, which captured many of those same powerful emotions. The network television program *20/20* chronicled the story of two Vietnamese children, presumed orphans, who had been evacuated when Saigon fell in 1975. Shelling from the advancing North Vietnamese army had separated this five- and four-year-old boy and girl from their parents, and everyone assumed the parents were dead. Actually the children's mother and father were alive, desperately searching for them. But nobody knew that, so the children were taken to the United States as orphans.

They grew up in loving American homes, with caring adoptive parents. The boy joined the United States Army and became a second lieutenant. His sister married and became the mother of three children. They kept in touch over the years, and in high school they had begun the painstaking research that eventually led them to discover their parents were alive after all.

Decades after the war, with relationships beginning to soften between Vietnam and the United States, the two children were finally granted visas to return and be reunited with their parents and the brothers and sisters they had never seen. Cameramen for *20/20* accompanied them, and the emotion captured by the cameramen was incredible.

Half a world separated this family—along with a terrible war, more than twenty years, and now even language. Yet they still had one thing in common. When they saw each other for the first time, they ran and fell into each other's arms with sobs, hugs, and kisses that said, in a language they all understood, "We love you. . . . We missed you. . . . We're so glad you're home."

They may have needed a translator to talk with each other in *words*, but as they sat and held hands, they clearly communicated the warmth and love that even a war couldn't kill.

THE PHYSICAL POWER OF TOUCH

While important symbolism accompanies our touch, it is not the only reason God made it a part of the blessing. Meaningful touch also communicates blessing on a very basic, physical level.

For one thing, over one-third of our five million touch receptors are centered in our hands![8] Our hands are so sensitive that some blind people are being taught to read without braille, by actually "seeing" through their fingertips! At Princeton University's Cutaneous Communication Laboratory, "vibratese" is an experimental procedure in translating the printed words into vibrations that can be perceived by fingertips.[9]

Interestingly enough, the act of laying on of hands, associated with the biblical blessing, has more recently become the focus of a great deal of secular interest and research. Dr. Dolores Krieger, a professor of nursing at New York University, has done numerous studies on the effects of laying on of hands. What she found is that both the toucher and the one being touched receive a psychological benefit from this practice.[10]

How is that possible? Inside our bodies is hemoglobin, the pigment of the red blood cells, which carries oxygen to the tissues. Repeatedly, Dr. Krieger has found that hemoglobin levels in *both* people's bloodstreams go up during the act of laying on of hands. As hemoglobin levels are invigorated, body tissues receive more oxygen. This increase of oxygen energizes a person and can even aid in the regenerative process if he or she is ill.

We are sure that Ephraim and Manasseh were not thinking, *Wow, our hemoglobin levels are going up!* when their grandfather laid his hands on them. However, one of the things that certainly stayed with them as they looked back on their day of blessing was the old patriarch's gentle touch.

Hugs and kisses were also a part of meaningful touching pictured in the Scriptures. So healthy is meaningful touch that we ought to listen to the words of Ralph Waldo Emerson: "I never like the giving of the hand, unless the entire body accompanies it!" Let's look further at the physical benefits of touching and the deep emotional needs that can be met by this first element of the family blessing.

How would you like to lower your husband's or wife's blood pressure? Protect your grade-school child from being involved in an immoral relationship later in life? Even add up to two years to your own life? (Almost sounds like an insurance commercial, doesn't it?) Actually, these are all findings in studies on the incredible power to bless found in meaningful touching.

MORE REASONS WHY MEANINGFUL TOUCH BLESSES US PHYSICALLY

Every day, researchers are discovering more and more information about the importance of touch. If we are serious about being a source of blessing to others, we must consider putting these important points into practice. As we saw in the studies of the laying on of hands, a number of physical changes take place when we reach out and touch.

A study at UCLA found, for example, that men and women need eight to ten meaningful touches a day just to maintain emotional and physical health.[11]

Gary once shared this information at a marriage seminar. As he talked about the "eight to ten meaningful touches," he noticed a man in the second row reach over and begin patting his wife on the shoulder and counting, "One, two, three . . ." That is *not* what the study meant by meaningful touch!

The UCLA researchers defined meaningful touch as a gentle touch, stroke, kiss, or hug given by significant people in our lives (a husband or wife, parent, close friend, and so on). They even estimated that if some type-A–driven men would hug their wives several times each day, they could increase their life spans by almost two years (not to mention the way it would improve their marriages)!

Obviously, we can physically bless those around us (and even ourselves) with meaningful touch. But touching does much more than that.

Do you have a newborn in your home? Newborns make tremendous gains if provided with meaningful touch—and may be at risk if they aren't.

Researchers at the University of Miami Medical School's Touch Research Institute began giving premature babies forty-five minutes of massage each day. Within ten days, the massaged babies showed 47 percent greater weight gain than those children who were not regularly touched.[12] A second study showed that actual bone growth of young children who had been deprived of parental touching was half that of children who received adequate physical attention.[13]

And in groundbreaking studies, Doctors Schanberg and Butler at Duke University Medical School found that without maternal touch, rat pups do not produce a type of protein crucial to their growth and development. When these rat pups were separated and unable to feel their mother's touch, they responded by slowly shutting down production of an enzyme crucial to the development of major organs. As soon as the pups were reunited with their mother, however, enzyme production returned to normal.[14]

Even the smallest act of touch can help a child who is unable to move. One group of physically handicapped children were placed on a smooth surface (like smooth Naugahyde) and a second group on a highly textured surface (like a rubber floor mat). EMG studies showed marked differences between the two groups, including increases in muscle tone simply from placing children on a textured surface.[15]

You can't get away from it. Overwhelming evidence shows that physical touch benefits and blesses children (and animals). But how about adults?

Are your parents getting up in years? Meaningful touch can be an important part of maintaining health and positive attitude in older persons. In a practice that has become commonplace now, residents in nursing homes were brought together with pets from a neighboring animal shelter. At first it was thought to be just a good recreational activity. Upon further study, more significant results began to surface. Those residents who had a pet to touch and hold not only lived longer than those without a pet; they also had a more positive attitude about life![16]

Elderly patients with more serious problems have also demonstrated a number of tremendous benefits from regular, meaningful touch. For those suffering with dementia, a regimen of regular meaningful touch significantly increased their nutritional intake, helping them gain needed weight.[17] In addition, with Alzheimer's patients, physical touch decreased strange movements and repetitive mannerisms such as picking up objects again and again.[18]

But perhaps the most powerful data to come out of research on aging concerns the ways touch may actually help preserve a healthy person's brain as it ages! Robert M. Stapolsky of Stanford University found that even a small amount of extra physical stimulation soon after birth made a lasting effect on rats' brains. Meaningful touch in infancy caused the rats' brains to put a brake on the development of glucocorticoids, stress hormones that are "a disaster to have in the bloodstream." As a result, when these rats became old, they didn't lose any of the 10 to 20 percent of memory-critical gray matter that older rats, monkeys, and humans normally tend to lose.[19]

While meaningful touch may not be the "fountain of youth," it certainly does provide a clear stream of physical benefits for young and old alike. And what's more, people who regularly give and receive meaningful touch consistently feel better about themselves and have higher self-worth.[20]

Meaningful Touch Blesses Our Relationships

An interesting study done at Purdue University demonstrates how important touch is in determining how we view someone else. Librarians at the school were asked by researchers to alternately touch and not touch the hands of students as they handed back their library cards. The experimenters then interviewed the students. Do you know what they found? You guessed it. Those who had been touched reported far greater positive feelings about both the library and the librarian than those who were not touched.[21]

A doctor I know, a noted neurosurgeon, did his own study on the effects of brief times of touch. With half his patients in the hospital, he would sit on their beds and touch them on the arm or leg when he came in to see how they were doing. With his remaining patients, he would simply stand near the bed to conduct his interview of how they were feeling.

Before the patients went home from the hospital, the nurses gave each patient a short questionnaire evaluating the treatment they received. They were especially asked to comment on the amount of time they felt the doctor had spent with them. While in actuality he had spent the same amount of time in each patient's room, those people he had come near and touched felt he had been in their room nearly twice as long as those he had not touched.

Other studies have shown similar results in very different circumstances. Shoppers in a Kansas City, Missouri, supermarket were asked to sample a new brand of pizza. Those who were touched for only a fraction of a second during the sales pitch were more likely to buy the new product.[22] And airline passengers who were touched "accidentally" by flight attendants on a long-distance flight rated those attendants as more qualified, the airline as more professional, and the plane trip *safer* than those who were not touched.[23]

Come on, Trent. Get serious, Smalley, you may be thinking. Do we really mean that a touch lasting a few seconds or less can help you build better relationships? Actually, we hope you can touch your loved ones much more than that, but even small acts of touch can indeed leave a lasting impression.

Touching a child on the shoulder when he or she walks in front of you, holding hands with your spouse while you wait in line, stopping for a moment to ruffle someone's hair—all these small acts can change how you are viewed by others and even how they view themselves. A ten-minute bear hug is not the only way to give another person the blessing. At times, the *smallest* act of touch can be a vehicle to communicating love and personal acceptance.

A freelance reporter from the *New York Times* once interviewed movie icon Marilyn Monroe. The reporter was aware of Marilyn's painful past and the fact that during her early years Marilyn had been shuffled from one foster home to another. The reporter asked Marilyn, "Did you ever feel loved by any of the foster families with whom you lived?"

"Once," Marilyn replied, "when I was about seven or eight. The woman I was living with was putting on makeup, and I was watching her. She was in a happy mood, so she reached over and patted my cheeks with her rouge puff. . . . For that moment, I felt loved by her."[24]

Marilyn Monroe had tears in her eyes when she remembered this event. Why? The touch lasted only a few seconds, and it happened years before. It was even done in a casual, playful way, not in an attempt to communicate great warmth or meaning. But as small an act as it was, it was like pouring buckets of love and security on the parched life of a little girl starved for affection.

Parents, in particular, need to know that neglecting to meaningfully touch their children starves them of genuine acceptance—so much so that it can drive them into the arms of someone else who is all too willing to touch them. Analyzing why some young people are drawn to cults, one author writes, "Cults and related movements offer a new family. They provide the follower with new people to worry about him, to offer him advice, to cry with him, and importantly, to hold him and touch him. Those can be unbeatable attractions."[25]

They certainly can, especially if meaningful touch has not been a part of the blessing a child receives. Even if a child is not lured into a cult to make up for years of touch deprivation, he or she can be drawn into the arms of an immoral relationship.

Promiscuous persons, prostitutes, and women who repeatedly have unwanted pregnancies have told researchers that their sexual activity is merely a way of satisfying yearnings to be touched and held. Dr. Marc Hollender, a noted psychiatrist, interviewed scores of women who have had three or more unwanted pregnancies. Overwhelmingly, these women said that they were "consciously aware that sexual activity was a price to be paid for being cuddled and held." Touching before intercourse was more pleasurable than intercourse itself, "which was merely something to be tolerated."[26]

A similar study with homosexual men indicated that they shared a common characteristic: the absence of meaningful touching by their fathers early in life.[27] Dr. Ross Campbell, in his excellent book *How to Really Love Your Child*, comes to a similar conclusion. He writes, "In all my reading and experience, I have never known one sexually disoriented person who had a warm, loving, and affectionate father."[28]

Touch from both a mother and father is important. If you are a single parent, your choice to provide appropriate touch is hugely important as well. Meaningful touching can protect a child from looking to meet this need in all the wrong places.

If we ignore the physical and emotional needs our children, spouse, or close friends have for meaningful touch, we deny them an important part of the blessing. What's more, we shatter a biblical guideline that our Lord Jesus himself set in blessing others.

LIVING THE BLESSING

Giving the Gift of Meaningful Touch

As we continue our look at appropriate, meaningful touch, write down your thoughts on whether you believe you are giving this essential element of the blessing to the important people in your life—especially children—right now. Why or why not? What would it take for you to learn to give this element of the blessing more often?

JESUS AND THE BLESSING OF MEANINGFUL TOUCH

Jesus was a model of someone who communicated the blessing to others. In fact, his blessing of children in the Gospels parallels the important elements of the family blessing, including meaningful touch. Let's look at Mark's account of that blessing.

> Then they brought little children to Him, that He might touch them; but the disciples rebuked those who brought them. But when Jesus saw it, He was greatly displeased and said to them, "Let the little children come to Me, and do not forbid them; for of such is the kingdom of God. . . ." And He took them up in His arms, laid His hands on them, and blessed them. (Mark 10:13–14, 16)

Meaningful touching was certainly a part of Christ's blessing as Mark described it. Mobbed by onlookers and protected by his disciples, Jesus could have easily waved to the children from a distance or just ignored them altogether. But he did neither. Jesus would not even settle for the politicians' "chuck under the chin" routine; he "took them up in His arms, laid His hands on them, and blessed them."

In this moment, Jesus was not simply communicating a spiritual lesson to the crowds. He could have done that by simply placing one child in the center of the group as he did on another occasion (Matt. 18:2). Here, Jesus was demonstrating his knowledge of the genuine importance of touch to a child.

For children, things become real when they are touched. Have you ever been to Disneyland and seen the look on little ones' faces when they come face-to-face with a person dressed like Goofy or Donald Duck? Even if they are initially fearful, soon they will want to reach out and touch the Disney character. This same principle allows children to stand in line for hours to see Santa Claus—the same children who normally can't stand still for five minutes.

Jesus was a master of communicating love and personal acceptance. He did so when he blessed and held these little children. But another time his sensitivity to the importance of touch played itself out more dramatically, when Jesus chose to touch a man who was barred by law from ever touching anyone again:

> And a leper came to Him, beseeching Him and falling on his knees before Him, and saying to Him, "If You are willing, You can make me clean."
>
> And moved with compassion, *He stretched out His hand, and touched him*, and said to him, "I am willing; be cleansed." And immediately the leprosy left him and he was cleansed. (Mark 1:40–42 NASB, italics added)

In Jesus' day, to touch a leper was unthinkable. Fear banished them from society, and people would not get within a stone's throw of them. In fact, they would throw stones at them if they did come close.[29] A parallel passage in Luke tells us that this man was "covered with leprosy." With their open sores covered by dirty bandages, lepers were the last persons anyone would want to touch. Yet the first thing Christ did when he met this man, even before he spoke to him, was to reach out his hand and *touch* him.

Can you imagine what that scene must have looked like? Think how this man must have longed for someone to touch him, not throw stones at him to drive him away. And remember, Jesus could have healed him first and then touched him. But recognizing his deepest need, Jesus stretched out his hand even before he spoke words of physical and spiritual healing.

I know of one person who could understand the pain of not being touched. Her name was Dorothy, and she spent years of her life longing for meaningful touch.

I learned about Dorothy through a speech teacher at a large, secular university, a man in his early sixties who is an outstanding Christian. For nearly twenty-five years, this man had been a source of encouragement to students inside and outside of class. Many young men and women have trusted Christ as their Savior through his quiet modeling of godly principles. However, what changed Dorothy's life was neither his ability to communicate nor his stirring class lectures, but one act of touch.

During the first day of an introductory speech class, this teacher was going around the room, having the students introduce themselves. Each student was to respond to the questions "What do I like about myself?" and "What don't I like about myself?"

Nearly hiding at the back of the room was Dorothy. Her long red hair hung down around her face, almost obscuring it from view. When it was Dorothy's turn to introduce herself, there was only silence in the room. Thinking perhaps she had not heard the question, the teacher moved his chair over near hers and gently repeated the question. Again, there was only silence.

Finally, with a deep sigh, Dorothy sat up in her chair, pulled back her hair, and in the process revealed her face. Covering nearly all of one side of her face was a large, irregularly shaped birthmark—nearly as red as her hair.

"That," she said, "should show you what I don't like about myself."

Moved with compassion, this godly professor did something he had never done before in a classroom. Prompted by God's Spirit, he leaned over and gave her a hug. Then he kissed her on her cheek where the birthmark was and said, "That's okay, honey, God and I still think you're beautiful."

Dorothy cried uncontrollably for almost twenty minutes. Soon other students had gathered around her and were offering their comfort as well. When she finally could talk, dabbing the tears from her eyes, she said to the professor, "I've wanted so much for someone to hug me and say what you said. Why couldn't my parents do that? My mother won't even touch my face."

Dorothy, just like the leper in Christ's time, had a layer of inner pain trapped beneath the outward scars. This one act of meaningful touching began to heal years of heartache and loneliness for Dorothy and opened the door that drew her to the Savior.

We know that for many people, meaningful touch simply wasn't a natural part of growing up. For me (John), growing up in Arizona, the cultural norm was, "It's okay to hug your horse, but not your kids!"

Wherever you live across the United States, you may

not come from a warm, affectionate background. Sociologist Sidney Jourand studied the touch behavior of pairs of people in coffee shops around the world. The difference between cultures was staggering. In San Juan, Puerto Rico, people touched on average 180 times per hour. In Paris, France, it was 110 times per hour. In Gainesville, Florida, 2 times per hour. And in London, England, 0 times per hour.[30]

We Americans aren't known as a country of huggers, and with all the media reports of child abuse and inappropriate touching, we have backed away from touch even more. We need to realize, however, that avoiding healthy, appropriate, meaningful touch sacrifices physical and emotional health in our lives and the lives of our loved ones.

If we want to be people who give the blessing to others, one thing is clear. Just like Isaac, Jacob, Jesus, and even the professor, we must include meaningful touch in our contacts with loved ones. This element of the blessing can lay the groundwork for the second key aspect of the blessing—a message that is put into words.

SEVEN

The Second Element: A Spoken Message

MOST OF US grew up reciting clever sayings like "Early to bed, early to rise, makes a man healthy, wealthy, and wise," "A bird in the hand is worth two in the bush," and "A stitch in time saves nine." But unlike all these words of wisdom, one saying we memorized is an absolute lie.

Do you remember the lines, "Sticks and stones may break my bones, but words will never hurt me"? That's not true, even a little! Words *can* hurt. They can cut a person deeply, destroy a friendship, rip apart a home or marriage, or devastate a child.

Words have incredible power to build us up or tear us down emotionally. This is particularly true when it comes to giving or gaining family approval. Many people can clearly remember words of praise their parents spoke years ago. Others can remember negative words they heard—and what their parents were wearing when they spoke them!

We should not be surprised, then, that the family bless-ing hinges on being a *verbalized* message. Abraham *spoke* a blessing to Isaac. Isaac *spoke* it to his son Jacob. Jacob *spoke* it to each of his twelve sons and to two of his grandchildren. Esau was so excited when he was called in to receive his bless-ing because, after years of waiting, he would finally *hear* the blessing. Later, the apostle Paul wrote eloquent words of bless-ing to growing churches all over the Roman Empire.

In the Scriptures, a blessing is not a blessing unless it is put into words and actually communicated.

THE POWER OF WORDS

If you are a parent, your children desperately need to receive *words* of blessing from you. If you are married, your wife or husband needs to receive *words* of love and acceptance on a regular basis. This very week with a friend, a coworker, or someone at your church, you will rub shoulders with some-one who needs to receive *words* of encouragement.

Throughout the Scriptures, we find a keen recognition of the power and importance of words. In the very beginning, God spoke and the world came into being (Gen. 1:3). When he sent us his Son to communicate his love and complete his plan of salvation, it was his *Word* that "became flesh and dwelt among us" (John 1:14). God has always been a God who communicates his blessing through words.

In the book of James, three word pictures grab our atten-tion and point out the power and importance of words. All three illustrate the ability the tongue (the primary conveyer of words) has to build up or break down relationships, the ability to bless or to curse.

First, the tongue is pictured as a "bit" used to direct a horse

(James 3:3). If you control a horse's mouth by means of a small bit, the entire animal will move in the direction you choose. (We have ridden a few horses that seem to be exceptions, but the general rule is certainly true.) The second picture illustrates this same principle in a different way. Here a "small rudder" is used to turn a great ship (3:4). These analogies point out the way words can direct and control a person or a relationship.

A parent, spouse, or friend can use this power of the tongue for good. He or she can steer a child away from trouble or provide guidance to a friend who is making an important decision. He or she can minister words of encouragement or lift up words of praise. But this power can also be misused, sometimes with tragic results.

That is what the third word picture shows us. It illustrates all too clearly that words can burn deeply into a person's life, often setting the course that person's future will take. Listen to the awesome power a verbalized message can have: "The tongue is a small part of the body, and yet it boasts of great things. Behold, how great a forest is set aflame by such a small fire! And the tongue is a fire, the very world of iniquity . . . and sets on fire the *course of our life*" (James 3:5–6 NASB, italics added).

Just like a forest fire, what we say to others can burn deeply into their hearts. In fact, I once saw a living picture of the darkness that can result from fiery words.

I first met Lynda on a blistering summer's day in Arizona. The temperature outside was over 105 degrees, and most people wore shorts or cool cotton clothing—but not Lynda. A tall, attractive twenty-year-old, she had on a heavy, long-sleeved *black* dress. In Arizona, people avoid wearing black during the summer because it soaks up the already scorching heat. Yet in talking with her in counseling over several weeks,

I found out that summer or winter, day or night, black was the only color Lynda would wear.

Lynda grew up with a cruel, abusive father who was addicted to alcohol and horror movies. As early as age five, Lynda was forced to stay in the family room and watch gruesome films. Her father would laugh hysterically when she cried in fear. As the years passed, he continued exposing her to other aspects of the occult. He finally died when Lynda was in high school, and the horror stopped . . . in part.

As Lynda and I talked, I realized it wasn't the pictures of terror that had covered Lynda's heart with such darkness. They were terrible without question. But it was her father's *words* that had done the most damage to her. For of all the hurtful things he did, what haunted her most was his favorite nickname for her. It came right out of his horror films: "demon daughter." That nickname burned its way into her heart and even affected the way she dressed on a searing summer day.

In the Scriptures there is tremendous power in a name. Before Moses went to Egypt to confront Pharaoh, he asked to know God's name. God changed Abram's name to Abraham, father of nations. Jesus changed Simon's name to Peter, a "rock." But leave it to an angry, evil father to change Lynda's name to one that represented darkness and death.

Thankfully, the ending to Lynda's story is one of great hope, not hurt. Through counseling and a loving church, she came to know Christ personally and traded in her old nickname for a new one: "child of God." As Jesus promised in the book of Revelation, "I will write on him [believers] the name of My God . . . My *new* name" (3:12, italics added). God's love broke through to Lynda's heart in a dramatic way. Today, Lynda is married to a devoted Christian man, wears a radiant smile, and has a wardrobe full of beautiful, pastel-colored clothes.

Perhaps you still stumble over hurtful words your parents, spouse, or a close friend once conveyed to you (or negative words you have communicated to yourself), words that come to memory time and again and point you in a direction in life you don't want to go. If so, don't lose hope. As you learn more about the blessing, you can begin to receive and give words that can lead to a new course of life.

Each of us should be keenly aware of the power of our words. We should also be aware of how powerful the *absence* of such words can be.

LIVING THE BLESSING

Words and You

As you consider this second element of the blessing, write down your thoughts about how you experienced this element in your early life. What was your dominant experience of words in your home growing up? Did you receive spoken (or written) words of blessing? Were words often used in hurtful ways—or simply not spoken? Was there a difference in how different adults in your life used (or didn't use) words? What part did spoken and written words play in whether or not you received the blessing as a child?

TODAY'S MOST COMMON CHOICE: "I'LL TELL THEM TOMORROW"

In homes like Lynda's, negative words can shatter children emotionally rather than shape them positively. But that is not the most common choice of parents. Most parents genuinely love their children and want the best for them. However, when it comes to sharing words of love and acceptance—words of blessing—they are up against an even more formidable foe than the temptation to communicate negative words.

A thief is loose in many homes today who masquerades as *fulfillment, accomplishment,* and *success.* This thief steals the precious gift of genuine acceptance from our children and leaves confusion and emptiness in its place. The villain's real name is *overactivity,* and it can keep parents so busy that the blessing is never shared, even with parents who dearly love their children, as one woman said, "Who has the time to stop and *tell* them?"

In many homes today both parents are working overtime, and a family night makes an appearance about as often as Halley's Comet. The result is, instead of Dad and Mom taking the time to communicate words of blessing, a babysitter named *silence* is left to mold a child's self-perception. Life is so hectic that, for many parents, that "just right" time to share a verbal blessing never quite comes around. What is the result?

A father tries to corner his son to communicate "how he feels about him" before he goes away to college, but now his son is too busy to listen.

A mother tries to communicate words of blessing to her daughter in the bride's room just before the wedding, but the photographer has to take her away to get that perfect shot.

Words of blessing should start in the delivery room and continue throughout life. Yet the "lack of time" and the thief's motto, "I'll have time to tell them tomorrow," rob the children of a needed blessing today.

"Oh, it's not that big a deal," you may say. "They know I love them and that they're special without my having to say it." Really? We wish that explanation worked with many of the people we counsel. To them, their parents' silence has communicated something far different from love and acceptance.

Let's look at what commonly happens in homes where

words of blessing are withheld. What we will see is that silence *does* communicate a message. Like an eloquent speech, it, too, can set a course for a person's life—but it's not the path most parents would like their children to take.

WHAT HAPPENS WHEN WE WITHHOLD WORDS OF BLESSING?

Both people and relationships suffer in the absence of words of love, encouragement, and support—words of blessing. Take marriage, for example.

Dr. Howard Hendricks, a noted Christian educator, likes to tell the story of a couple who had been married more than twenty years, but whose problems had become so acute they were now considering a divorce. Dr. Hendricks asked the husband, "When was the last time you told your wife you loved her?" The man glared at him, crossed his arms, and said, "I told my wife I loved her on our wedding day, and it stands until I revoke it!"

Take a guess what was destroying that marriage. When words of blessing are withheld in a marriage, unmet needs for security and acceptance act like sulfuric acid and eat away at a relationship.

Not only marriages, but individuals—and particularly children—suffer from the lack of a verbal blessing. Without words of love, acceptance, and encouragement, children often grow up traveling one of two roads that lead to unhealthy extremes.

The Road of Overachievement

Dan grew up in a home where nothing positive was ever said. In fact, little of *anything* was ever said. His parents seemed too busy with their careers or too preoccupied with constantly remodeling the house to do much talking. There came, however, an exception to the general rule of verbal indifference when Dan was just a boy.

At the end of one semester in grade school, Dan received an excellent report card with nearly all As. For the first time in his memory, his parents openly praised him. At last, he felt like somebody.

Like a starving man who stumbles across a loaf of bread, Dan thought he had learned the key to hearing words of acceptance: overachieve. To him, it was worth the hours spent inside studying (with the neighbor kids playing right outside his window) just to hear a few words of affirmation at the end of each semester.

This working to overachieve lasted right through college and beyond, taking his motivation to "show them I'm somebody" right into the marketplace. He quickly found a job and became a *perfect* junior executive—which translated means he was a committed workaholic, always driven to achieve more and more, regardless of the personal or relationship costs.

Why the intense drive and the insatiable need to achieve? Just look back at Dan's home, where words of blessing were given only for spectacular achievement. Dan would never admit it (though inside he always knew), but pulling into his parents' driveway in a new car said he was still somebody—didn't it? Getting that corner office would show them—wouldn't it?

Dan had fallen into the trap many men and women do who never received the blessing. Like Moses' fading glory, his accomplishments could not provide his missing sense of personal acceptance—at least not for long. Dan was forever having to make one more deal, sell one more product, attend one more motivational seminar. Unsaid words of love and acceptance in his early life made him a driven man.

Dan finally did come to grips with missing out on the blessing and learned to find a little more balance in his life. Until then, however, his search for personal acceptance kept him on the barren road to workaholism and overachievement.

The Road of Withdrawal

Dan's type of drivenness is one common response to missing out on words of blessing. But many people head in the opposite direction. Convinced they can do nothing to hear words of love and acceptance, they give up and travel down the road of apathy, depression, and withdrawal—where a terrifying, yet beckoning, cliff awaits.

A classic example of a child who took this road is found in a film that circulated a few decades ago. As the movie begins, we see several children waiting for their school bus. The sun is out on a cold January morning. Snow covers the rural country-side like a beautiful, white blanket.

All bundled up for winter weather, a few of the children are making snowballs and throwing them at a fence. Others laugh and talk and stomp their feet to stay warm. All except Cliff.

Standing by himself at the edge of the group, Cliff stares down at the ground. In the next few moments, you almost get the feeling that Cliff is invisible. Several other children run right by him in excited conversation; others crowd around him when the bus finally comes. But Cliff never looks up, and the other children never speak to him or acknowledge his existence.

The children rush to see who gets on the school bus first. Glad to be in out of the cold, the children happily take their seats—that is, all except Cliff. The last one on the bus, he wearily mounts the steps as if climbing each one requires a monumental effort. He stops briefly and looks up expectantly into the faces of the other children, but no one beckons him to join them. Heaving a sigh, he slumps into a seat behind the driver.

There is a whoosh of compressed air from the bus's hydraulic system. The door slams shut. With one look behind him to make sure everything is in order, the driver pulls slowly away from the curb and onto the country lane.

They have traveled only a few miles when suddenly Cliff drops his books and staggers to his feet. Standing next to the bus driver, steadying himself on a metal pole, the boy has a wild and distant look in his eyes. Shocked by Cliff's sudden ill appearance, the bus driver asks, "Are you all right? Are you sick or something? Kid, what's the matter?" Cliff never answers, and half out of frustration, half out of concern, the bus driver pulls over to the side of the road and opens the door.

Cliff begins to walk down the steps of the bus, then pitches forward and crumples into the snow. The opening scene ends with the driver standing over Cliff's prone body, trying to figure out what has happened. As the camera pulls away, we hear an ambulance siren begin to whine in the distance, but somehow you know its coming will be too late.

This scene is from the hard-to-find but excellent educational film *A Cipher in the Snow,* a film that is designed for teachers but speaks to anyone concerned about giving the blessing to others. It is based on a true story of a young boy who actually died on the way to school one day and the resulting confusion over the reasons.

Medical records indicated no history of problems in either Cliff or his family. Even the autopsy shed no light on his death. Only after an interested teacher looked into his school and family background were the reasons for his death discovered.

This teacher found that Cliff's life had been systematically erased like a blackboard. In his first few years at school, he had done well, up until problems began at home. His parents' marriage had disintegrated, and a new, preoccupied stepfather never had time or interest to fill any of the missing gaps. Resentful of any attention his new wife gave Cliff, the stepfather would limit their time together. His mother loved Cliff dearly, but soon she was either too busy or too intimidated by her new husband to give the boy any attention at all. Like someone pushed away from a seat near the fireplace, Cliff was now left with only the cold ache of indifference.

As a reaction to his home life, Cliff's schoolwork began to suffer. Homework assignments were turned in late or not at all. Tired of his apparent apathy, his teachers gave up on him and left him to work alone. Cliff also began to withdraw from the other children at school, and he lost the few friends he once had. He would not begin a conversation, and soon other children wouldn't bother to try. Slowly but surely, he retreated into a world of silence.

In only a few months, everything and everyone of value to Cliff had either been lost or taken from him. With no place of shelter and no words of encouragement, he felt like a cipher—an empty zero. This sensitive child was unable to stand the pain for long.

Cliff was not killed by an infirmity or a wound. He was killed by the lack of spoken love and acceptance. Cliff withstood the painful silence as long as he could. Ultimately, however, the lack of a spoken blessing from family and friends acted like a deadly cancer. After months of pursuing its course, it finally ate away his will to live. He died a cipher in the snow, believing he was totally alone and unwanted.

WORDS MATTER

Are words or their absence *really* that powerful? Solomon thought so. His words are like ice water in our faces, shocking us into reality: "Death and life are in the power of the tongue" (Prov. 18:21).

If we struggle with communicating words of love and acceptance to our families or friends, another proverb should encourage us. Again, it is Solomon writing: "Do not withhold good from those to whom it is due, when it is in the power of your hand to do so. Do not say . . . 'Go, and come back, and tomorrow I will give it,' when you have it with you" (Prov. 3:27–28).

If we can open our mouths to talk, we have the ability to communicate the blessing through spoken words. As we will see, writing out words of blessing can be equally powerful, especially when spoken words aren't possible. In fact, written words of blessing have their own special advantage in that they can be composed more carefully and deliberately and can be kept and reread.

WHY IS IT SO HARD TO EXPRESS WORDS OF BLESSING?

The damage of withholding words of blessing should be obvious in the examples of Lynda, Dan, and Cliff. But if words of love and acceptance are so important, why are they offered so infrequently? Here are a few reasons we have gathered from people we have counseled:

- "I don't want to inflate my child's ego."
- "I'm afraid if I praise them, they'll take advantage of me and won't finish their work."

86

- "Communication is too much like work. I work all day, then she expects me to work all night talking to her."
- "I just don't know what to say."
- "They know I love them without my having to say it."
- "If I get started, I'll have to make a habit of it."

Then there's our personal favorite:

- "Telling children their good points is like putting on perfume. A little is okay, but put on too much, and it stinks."

As far as we are concerned, it's that statement that stinks. And none of those explanations come anywhere close to the real reason many people hesitate to bless their children or others with words of love and acceptance.

The real reason most people withhold this part of the blessing is that their parents never gave it to them.

LIVING THE BLESSING

Speaking Words of Blessing

Write out your thoughts about how you currently give this element of the blessing to important people in your life. Are you generally comfortable in speaking words of praise and affirmation to a child (or to anyone else)? If not, what holds you back from doing so? Do any of the excuses or family rules listed in this chapter sound familiar—or can you think of any more? Do you find some people in your life easier to praise than others? What are some strategies that could make communicating words of blessing a little easier?

The Danger of Family Rules

Both praise and criticism seem to trickle down through generations. That means if you never heard words of love and acceptance, you can expect to struggle with sharing them yourself. Why? It's as if your family had a rule that loving words were best left unsaid, and you may find it very difficult to break this rule.

Every family operates by certain rules, spoken or unspoken, that prescribe "the way our family does things." Some families have a rule that "people who know anything about anything" open Christmas presents on Christmas *morning*. Other families follow the rule that "truly civilized people" open Christmas presents on Christmas *Eve*. (Cindy just groaned when we wrote this!) Conflicting family rules often meet in a marriage. Many an argument has gone fifteen rounds to see whose family rule will win out in a new marriage.

Families set all kinds of rules: what we will eat in this family and what we won't eat. What television programs we can watch and which are dull or off-limits. What is safe to talk about and what subjects should never be brought up. Whom we invite over to the house and who doesn't get an invitation.

In some cases family rules can be very helpful. For example, families can adopt biblical rules like not letting the sun go down on anger and being kind, one to another. Another way of setting positive family rules is by using contracts that can help build communication and encourage children.[1] These types of family guidelines can be safely passed down generation after generation.

But not all family rules are worth retaining. In fact, some can devastate a family. Like words cast in steel, a destructive family rule can hammer away at a family from parent to son or daughter. The process will continue from generation to generation until at last someone breaks this painful pattern—someone like Cheryl.

When Cheryl was growing up, a simple plaque hung in the family room. The plaque had belonged to Cheryl's grandfather and had become a kind of unspoken family motto. The plaque was not impressive looking, and it carried only two hand-painted words: *Stand Up.* Just two words—yet these two words had written volumes of hurt into three generations of Cheryl's family.

The words had originally been part of a longer sentence, a motto that went something like this: "Don't take anything off anyone. Stand up and fight." This may have been a helpful frontier slogan, but it did nothing but damage personal relationships in Cheryl's family.

Just look at Cheryl's father, who had been infected with the never-give-an-inch attitude of *his* father. "I'm sorry" or "You're right" were not in the vocabulary of someone who based his life on the words *stand up and fight.* Also absent were any words that were not useful in a fight—words like *I love you, Will you forgive me?* and *You're important to me.* While following this never-give-an-inch family rule pushed Cheryl's father ahead in business, it pushed him back into a corner with his wife and children.

Cheryl's mother and father fought constantly, each an expert on the other's faults, neither willing to give an inch in an argument. When each of Cheryl's four brothers and sisters grew old enough to dislike taking orders from their father, they joined the battle too. Soon there were seven people under the same roof following the family rule of Stand Up and Fight and its corollary principles, Fight for My Rights and Death

Before Saying I'm Sorry. This situation persisted until Cheryl became a Christian.

Cheryl went away to a Life camp and trusted Christ as her Lord and Savior. The first thing she noticed when she came back home was that plaque: Stand Up. She thought about how Jesus had laid down his life and how tired she was of following this family rule. Little by little and at the painful cost of constant ridicule from her brothers and sisters, Cheryl began to break several family rules.

Right in the middle of a fight, for instance, Cheryl would say, "I'm sorry; you're right. Would you forgive me?" and end the argument. She even began saying, "Love you, Mom; love you, Dad" and then giving her parents a hug as she left for school.

Cheryl's father had never gotten the blessing from his parents, only a plaque that almost destroyed his marriage and family. But over the next two years, he received the blessing from Cheryl. Meaningful touch, words of high value, the picture of a future filled with hope, and the commitment to love him no matter the cost—all these were relationship tools that chipped away at the existing family structure.

Family rules die hard, but they can be broken. Cheryl's younger sister was so taken with Cheryl's changed life that she also trusted Christ. Soon Cheryl's older brother followed, and the plaque on the wall was beginning to shake. Last Christmas, as a baby Christian, her father took down the plaque.

What a testimony to God's power to break even the most difficult family rule. And what a help to Cheryl's family to have a new family rule to follow. They are now free to speak up and share words of blessing with each other—because of one child's courage to go to battle with a hurtful rule and dare to speak words of blessing.

PUTTING WORDS
OF BLESSING INTO PRACTICE

We put words of blessing into practice in our homes and relationships by deciding to speak up rather than clam up. Good intentions aside, good words are needed to bestow the blessing on a child, spouse, or friend.

Note that we are not simply saying, "*Talk more* to your children or others." While talking is normally a good idea, sometimes if you don't know how to communicate in a positive way, you can say less by saying more. As we will see in the next chapter, it is not just *any* words, but words of high value, that attach themselves to a person and communicate the blessing. These are the kinds of words you often hear in the final hours before a family reunion ends.

Almost all of us have had the opportunity to attend a family reunion. A common phenomenon at these gatherings is that during the first two days, everyone is busy talking up a storm about this recipe, that football team, this book they've read, or that movie to attend. But something happens the last afternoon of the reunion. Suddenly, with only an hour left before family members say their good-byes, meaningful words will begin to be spoken.

A brother will say in private to his sister, "I know things will work out in your marriage. I'll be praying for you." An aunt will say to her niece, "You've always made me proud. I know school is hard, but I also know you can do it. I believe in you." Or a daughter will say to a parent, "Look around you, Mom. We didn't turn out half bad, did we? We have you and Dad to thank."

So often, we seem to need the pressure of time before we say things closest to our hearts. But when it comes to your children, your spouse, your close friends, even with your parents, it may be later than you think. In some relationships, it is already late afternoon in your opportunity to talk to those you love.

In 1986 a tragic plane crash in Japan took the lives of more than five hundred people. The four people who survived the crash told authorities and reporters the story of their doomed flight. For the last thirty-four minutes, the plane flew erratically, without a rear tail stabilizer to control their descent, and this half hour was a time of panic and horror for all on board. Some passengers cried in fear. Others took the time to don life jackets. But one middle-aged Japanese man, Hirotsugu Kawaguchi, took his last few moments to write a note to his family. Rescuers at the wreckage site found the note on his body, and it finally made its way to his wife and three children.

Listen to the last words of this man, who deeply loved his family. They picture his desire for his wife and children to have a special future, even now that they would be physically separated in this life.

> I'm very sad, but I'm sure I won't make it. The plane is rolling around and descending rapidly. There was something like an explosion that has triggered smoke. . . . Ysuyoshi [his oldest son], I'm counting on you. You and the other children be good to each other, and work hard. Remember to help your mother. . . . Keiko [his wife], please take good care of yourself and the children. To think our dinner last night was our last. I am grateful for the truly happy life I have enjoyed. [2]

Hirotsugu Kawaguchi died when the plane crashed. His wife and children no longer have him to hold and love. But they do have his final words to them, words that pictured his hopes for their future, words that will echo in their lives in a positive way in the years to come.

Ask any family who has watched a son or daughter go off to war. We hang on to words from them. We long to get our words of love and prayers for their safety to them. Words carry the blessing, and in the next chapter, you can learn about the kind of words—words of high value—that can especially bless people.

But don't delay. Time passes so quickly. Please don't let that important person leave your life without receiving the second element of the blessing—the spoken (or written) word.

[EIGHT]

The Third Element:
Attaching High Value

DIANE'S PARENTS HAD tried unsuccessfully for years to have children. Perhaps that is one reason why their joy was unbounded when they learned that they were expecting their first child. Everything seemed fine during the pregnancy and delivery . . . until they saw the doctor's reaction. When Diane was given to them for the first time, they saw that her left arm had never developed below the elbow.

There were tears in the delivery room and deep concern as test after test was performed on Diane. As doctors and specialists sought to determine the extent of her physical problems, Diane's parents wondered how to handle the anxious questions from relatives and friends.

Two days later the doctors told Diane's parents some encouraging news. In all their tests, they had not detected any other problems. With the exception of her left arm, Diane appeared to be a normal, healthy baby girl.

After the doctors had gone, Diane's parents bowed together in prayer. They thanked God that their daughter had no other serious problems. But they prayed something else that would prove to be of tremendous benefit to their daughter. In that hospital room, with Diane nestled in her mother's arms, her parents prayed that their love for her would make up for any physical disabilities she possessed. They decided that morning that they would encourage Diane to become all that God would have her be, in spite of the problems they and Diane would have to face along the way.

Years have gone by since Diane's parents prayed for her in that hospital room, and their prayer has been answered in many ways. Diane went through high school with honors and attended a major university. Even today, something special about Diane draws your attention away from her empty sleeve, particularly when you listen to her play a beautiful melody on the piano—with only one hand.

Diane has faced tremendous obstacles in her life: the stares, giggles, and tactless questions from her peers in grade school; the fears and uncomfortable feelings of whether to go to a dance in junior high; the questions and worry that perhaps she would never date in high school or college—just to name a few. However, despite the real struggles of being born with a handicap, Diane received a precious and powerful gift from her parents: the security of knowing she was highly valued and unconditionally accepted.

"My parents didn't try to hide from me the fact that I was different," Diane told us. "They have been very realistic with me. But I always knew, and they have told me over and over, that I am their 'greatest claim to fame.' Whether I was trying out for softball or my dad was teaching me how to drive, they have been my biggest fans. They have prayed for me and thought the best, even when I've pouted and gotten angry at God because of my handicap. Without question, my parents deserve a lot of credit for helping me accomplish the things I have."

They certainly do deserve credit for deciding, in spite of a physical loss, to value their daughter as whole and complete. Diane's parents are realists. They have never sugarcoated the very real problem their daughter has faced. But all her life, they have communicated the blessing to her by showering her with meaningful touch and words of high value and unconditional acceptance.

Words of High Value

What do we mean by "high value"? Let's look at the word *value* to see the part it plays in the blessing.

To value something means to attach great importance to it. This is at the very heart of the concept of blessing. As you saw in chapter 4, the root word for *blessing* carries the dual meaning of "bow the knee" and to "add value." In relationship to God the word came to mean "to adore with bended knees."[1] Bowing before someone is a graphic picture of valuing that person.

Notice the important principle here: anytime we bless someone, we are attaching high value to him or her. Let's illustrate this by an example Gary liked to share when his children were young.

"In my life, I want God to be of utmost value to me. He is my best friend and the source of my life. If I were to chart this on a 1-to-10 scale, I would value the Lord at a 10, of highest value. Right beneath my relationship with the Lord would come my relationship with Norma, my wife. Humanly speaking, she is my best friend, and I love and value her right beneath my love for the Lord—maybe a 9.5. Then come my children. I love each of them dearly, and while neither they nor Norma are aware that I love them at different levels, I would value them at about a 9.4, right behind Norma. I do not love them less, but in attaching value to them, they come right behind my relationship with my Lord and with my wife.

"Emotionally there are times with the kids when my feelings might drop to a 6.4 or even a 4.2—particularly if we are camping in our mini mobile home and it has been raining all week. But, because I want to love and value them at a 9.4, I continually try to push their value back where it belongs. The same thing is true with Norma. I don't want to hurt or devalue her in any way. That is why, if I do offend her, I immediately decide to raise her value to just beneath where I value the Lord."

LIVING THE BLESSING

Were You Valued?

As you read about this element of the blessing, consider: How important did you feel in your home when you were growing up? In what ways did the adults in your life show—or not show—that they valued you? Can you think of a story about a time when you really felt special? When you felt you didn't matter? How did that sense of being valued or not valued affect your present life?

How does that idea of choosing to raise a person's value—even in challenging circumstances—apply to the blessing?

It bears repeating that when we bless someone, we are

deciding—choosing—to hold on to the fact that he or she is of high value. That is what the psalmist is telling us in Psalm 103:1 when he says, "Bless the LORD, O my soul; and all that is within me, bless His holy name!" When we "bless the Lord," we are actually recognizing God's intrinsic worth and attaching high value to him. We are saying that he is worthy of our bowing the knee to him.[2]

In the Scriptures, we are often called on to bless or value the Lord, but the Scriptures also give many examples of humans blessing other humans (Deut. 33:1–2; Josh. 14:13; 2 Sam. 6:18; and others). When they did, each was attaching high value to the person he was blessing, recognizing him or her as a very special individual.

This is exactly what the patriarchs in the Old Testament were doing when they extended the family blessing to their children—attaching high value to them. We do the same when we bless our children, spouses, or friends. This concept of valuing another person is so important that we believe it can be found at the heart of every healthy relationship. Every person needs the blessing to feel truly loved and secure about himself or herself.

WORDS OF HIGH VALUE IN OLD TESTAMENT HOMES

In the Old Testament, shining threads of love and value run through the fabric of the blessing. Remember Isaac's word picture, "Surely, the smell of my son is like the smell of a field which the LORD has blessed" (Gen. 27:27)? But Jacob understood exactly what his father meant by that. So can you if you remember driving through the country when hay or wheat has been harvested recently. Particularly with the morning dew on the ground, or after a rain shower, the smell of a newly cut field is as fresh and refreshing as a mountain spring.

Isaac also pictured his son as someone whom other people, including his own family, should greatly respect. "Let peoples serve you," he said, "and nations bow down to you."

In the United States today, no premium is placed on physically bowing before dignitaries. About the only people who know how to bow anymore are actors and orchestra conductors. Most of us would have to practice for hours to properly bow if we were going to meet a visiting king or queen. In Isaac's day, however, bowing was a mark of respect and honor, something that was expected in the presence of an important person.

We can't miss the idea in these two pictures of praise that Isaac thought his son was very valuable, someone who had great worth. This message is exactly what modern-day children need to hear from their parents. It's what Diane heard from her parents, the message that caused her life to blossom and grow in spite of her physical deformity.

THE KEY TO COMMUNICATING VALUE

Telling children they are valuable can be difficult for many parents, especially if the parents never heard such words when they themselves were young. Besides, as we saw in a previous chapter, that just-right time to say such important words can get crowded out by the urgent demands of a busy schedule.

Some children do hear the obligatory "I love you" during holidays or at the airport, but it seems stiff and out of place.

Other children (like Dan in chapter 7) may hear an occasional word of praise, but only if they perform well on a task. When words of value are only linked to a child's efforts to obtain a blessing, the child retains a nagging uncertainty about whether he or she ever really received it. If his or her performance ever drops even a small amount, that child may ask and ask again, "Am I loved for who I am or only for what I can do?"

We need to find a better way to communicate a message of high value and acceptance, a way to express a person's valuable qualities and character traits apart from his or her performance. Hidden inside the family blessing is a key to communicating such feelings to our children, spouses, friends, or church families, a key that we can perfect with only a little practice and that even gets around the walls a defensive adult or child can set up. This key is found in the way word pictures are used throughout the Scriptures.

THE POWER OF A PICTURE

We may not be aware of it, but we use word pictures all the time. Let me give you one example that I remember vividly.

I was at lunch some time ago with a close friend in Dallas, Texas. We were eating at a quaint little basement restaurant where you walk down a steep flight of steps to reach the front door. The hostess seated us, and from our table we had a view of the stairs leading down to the restaurant.

While we waited for our meal, we noticed at the top of the stairs a little girl of about two. She was holding the hand of someone we could not completely see. In fact, all we could see were two huge tennis shoes and a massive hand that totally engulfed the little girl's. As these two came down the stairs, we were able to see more and more of this very large man helping his little daughter down the stairs.

When they reached the foot of the stairs and the door to the restaurant opened, in walked a football player for the Dallas Cowboys. At six-foot-four and 265 pounds, this huge defensive tackle took up nearly the whole doorway. As he and his daughter walked by our table (the ground shaking and plates rattling as he passed), my friend leaned over to me and said, "Boy, what a moose!"

Calling this man a moose is using a word picture. Hall of Fame tackle Randy White does not have antlers and fur, and while he is very large as far as human beings go, he does not outweigh even a baby moose. Yet when my friend pictured him as a moose (out of his hearing, of course), I instantly understood: a very large individual was walking by our table!

Most of us do this all the time. We use word pictures to convey an emotional feeling apart from the literal meaning of the words. For instance, some politically incorrect men have called attractive women "chicks" down through the years. Obviously, they do not refer to the fact that the women scratch around in the dirt. A junior high school girl who tells her girlfriends that her latest boyfriend is a "dream" at a slumber party does not mean he will evaporate when she wakes up (even if it frequently happens!).

Positive or negative, word pictures are a useful communication tool because they are vivid and easy for most people to understand. They have an emotional impact that ordinary words may lack. That's why word pictures are so effective in giving a blessing.

We can see this clearly in the blessing Jacob used with three of his sons. Each is a beautiful example of how this communication tool can be used to attach high value to a child.

Jacob picked a different word picture for each of his sons to bestow the blessing on them. We read, "And this is what their father said to them when he blessed them. He blessed them, every one with the blessing appropriate to him" (Gen. 49:28 NASB).

Judah is a lion's [cub] . . . and as a lion, who dares rouse him up? (Gen. 49:9 NASB)

Judah was depicted as a lion's cub. In the Scriptures a lion portrayed strength, and the lion was also a symbol of royalty in the ancient Near East.[3] Judah's leadership qualities and strength of character were illustrated by this picture.

Naphtali is a doe let loose, he gives beautiful words. (Gen. 49:21 NASB)

Jacob pictured Naphtali as a doe. The grace and beauty of this gentle animal were used to show the artistic qualities this son possessed. He was the one who spoke and wrote beautiful words.

Joseph is a fruitful bough, a fruitful bough by a spring. (Gen. 49:22 NASB)

Joseph was described as a fruitful bough by a spring. This word picture illustrated how Joseph's unfailing trust in the Lord allowed him to provide a place of refuge for his family. Jacob's word picture carries a similar message to one used first of Jesus in Psalm 1:3: "And he will be like a tree firmly planted by streams of water, which yields its fruit in its season, and its leaf does not wither; and in whatever he does, he prospers" (NASB).

Each of Jacob's sons was an individual, and each of them received a blessing that depicted his value to his father in the form of a word picture he could remember always. It's an example we would do well to follow when we give the blessing. But before we rush off to call our child or spouse a lion, doe, or fruitful bough, we need to learn a little more about word pictures.

To do so, let's turn to a book in the Old Testament that is filled with them. While this book pictures a marriage relationship, the same principles can be used in giving children—or anyone else—the blessing. Let's look in on how this couple communicated words of love, acceptance, and praise. In doing so, we will discover four keys to communicating high value.

WORD PICTURES: FOUR KEYS TO COMMUNICATING HIGH VALUE

In the Song of Solomon, God's picture of an ideal courtship and marriage, a loving couple praises each other using word pictures more than eighty times in eight short chapters. That's a lot! But they had a lot they wanted to communicate about how highly they valued each other and their relationship.

Let's begin our look at how they used these descriptive words with each other by looking in on their wedding night. Not often is someone's wedding night written up for posterity, but this one is worth remembering. It is a vivid record of a loving, godly relationship.[4]

Seven times (the biblical number of perfection) Solomon praises his bride, who was altogether beautiful to him. He begins his praise of her by saying, "Behold, you are fair, my love! Behold, you are fair! You have dove's eyes behind your veil" (Song 4:1).

Key #1: Use an Everyday Object

What Solomon did with this word picture (and what a wise parent does in blessing his or her child) was to use an everyday object to capture a character trait or physical attribute of his beloved. In this case, he pictured her eyes as those of a dove. The gentle, shy, and tender nature of these creatures would be familiar to his bride. By picturing this familiar animal, Solomon was able to communicate far more meaning than he could by using words. (Words themselves are often one-dimensional, but a word picture can be multidimensional.) An added feature is that each time she saw a dove thereafter, she would be reminded of how her husband viewed her and valued her.

The parents of one young woman we know shared a similar kind of familiar word picture in blessing to their daughter. Emma was born in late December, near Christmas Day. As she grew older, her parents would repeatedly say to her, "Just remember, you're God's special Christmas gift to us, a gift of great price because you're so special to us." As an illustration of their feelings, each Christmas a small package would appear next to the Christmas tree, addressed from Jesus to Emma's parents. Each year Emma would be given the honor of opening this package, which always contained her baby picture and a reminder that she was her parents' Christmas gift. Last we heard, this had been going on for more than thirty-five years and not just at Christmas.

Listen to Emma's thoughts about how this word picture has ministered to her:

"There have been many times when I haven't felt very special. I can remember one time in particular. It was my thirtieth birthday, and I was struggling with growing older. When I was at my lowest point, I received a package in the mail from my parents. In the package was a brightly wrapped box, and inside was my baby picture and a note from my parents. I've always known I was special to them. But I *needed* to know I was special that day. It wasn't even Christmas, but reading again that I was their special 'Christmas gift' and very special to them—even on my thirtieth birthday—filled my heart with love and warmth."

Key #2: *Match the Emotional Meaning of the Trait You Are Praising with the Object You've Picked*

Over and over Solomon used everyday objects that captured the emotional meaning behind the trait he wanted to praise. These objects may not be familiar to us, but they were familiar to his bride. Take, for example, his praise for his beloved just a few verses later. He looks at his bride and says, "Your neck is like the tower of David, built for an armory, on which hang a thousand bucklers, all shields of mighty men" (4:4).

Was Solomon trying to end his marriage before it began? Certainly not. Let's look at just how meaningful this analogy would have been to an insecure, blushing bride on her wedding night.

High above the old city of Jerusalem stood the Tower of David. A farmer working outside the city walls could look up from his work and see this imposing structure. What would impress him—even more than the height of this tower—was what hung from it.

Hanging on the tower during times of peace were the war shields of David's "mighty men"—King David's greatest warriors and the leaders of his armies. The sun shining off their shields would be a reassuring sight for one outside the protection of the city walls. By the same token, if that farmer looked up and saw that the shields of the mighty men had been taken off the tower, he would know it was time to hightail it inside the city walls! Danger was in the land.

Solomon's comparing his bride's neck to David's tower

now begins to make a little more sense. In Old Testament times a person's neck stood for his or her appearance *and* attitude. That is why the Lord would call a disobedient Israel a "stiff-necked people" (Ex. 33:5). For Solomon, the peace and security represented in David's tower provided a powerful illustration to express his love for his bride. He was praising the way she carried herself—with serenity and security.[5]

Let's look at a modern-day example to reinforce what we have discovered about this kind of word picture, something that took place in my home.

For the first four years of her life, our daughter Kari had our undivided attention. So it's understandable that there were adjustments for all of us when a precious baby named Laura came home with Cindy from the hospital.

While there were times when Kari felt envious of all the attention the new baby demanded, she still tried her best to be the perfect big sister. She would run to get a diaper for Mommy or tiptoe down the hall on those rare occasions when the baby was napping. Or she would simply sit next to Cindy when she was feeding the baby, stroking Laura's little head or holding her dainty little fingers.

Cindy noticed and appreciated our older daughter's efforts, and she wanted to find a creative way to communicate high value to Kari. She looked around for an object that would represent some of the same qualities she saw in Kari. She found it one day while they were watching television.

While feeding the baby that day, Cindy and Kari enjoyed a *National Geographic* afternoon special about eagles in Alaska. The breathtaking footage included a long scene where a beautiful mother eagle helped to feed, protect, and shelter her young. There was the picture that Cindy had been looking for. On a trip by a local toy store, she bought a small, inexpensive stuffed eagle and waited for a quiet time to talk with Kari.

"Sweetheart," she said, "do you remember watching that television program about the eagles?"

Instantly Kari recalled many of the details and talked about how much she liked the program.

"Well, honey, I want you to know that you remind me of that mommy eagle. You've helped take such good care of your little sister since she's come home—even when it hasn't been easy—and I want you to know how proud I am of you."

For *days* Kari carried that stuffed eagle around with her, never letting it out of her arms. It was the first thing I saw when I got home that night and the only stuffed animal she allowed to sleep with her at bedtime.

By using an object familiar to Kari to praise her, Cindy wisely communicated more than a simple compliment. She gave our daughter a living—or at least a stuffed—illustration of one way she was so valuable to her mother.

LIVING THE BLESSING

Communicating High Value

Now is a good time to consider how effective you are in conveying a message of high value to your children or other important people in your life. Write out your thoughts on this. Brainstorm three different word pictures (using the four keys listed in this chapter) that you could use to communicate to an important person in your life that he or she is very special to you. If you are currently in a situation where someone you love is feeling insecure or defensive, how could you use word pictures to make the situation better and improve your relationship?

Key #3: Use Word Pictures That Unravel Defenses

Solomon took advantage of a third aspect of word pictures: the ability to get around the defenses of people who, for one reason or another, have a hard time hearing. This quality is something that a parent, spouse, or friend can use today. Whether we are dealing with defensive people or those who battle with insecurity, using a word picture can help us get around their resistance and communicate high value to them.

Let's look first at how a word picture can encourage an insecure person. We can see this with Solomon's bride herself, known in Song of Solomon as the Shulamite woman.

Like most young women who would unexpectedly meet a dashing young king, the Shulamite woman was insecure about her appearance. When she first met Solomon she said, "Do not look upon me, because I am dark, because the sun has tanned me" (Song 1:6). But after she had been around Solomon for only a short time, she called herself "the rose of Sharon, and the lily of the valleys" (2:1). That is quite a change of perspective! How did it happen?

It happened because Solomon's word pictures made their way around his bride's defenses. If Solomon had simply said, "You're cute," her insecurity could have thrown up a dozen reasons why this matter-of-fact statement could not be true: "Maybe his eyesight is bad." "I bet he's been hunting for three months, and I'm the first woman he's seen." "Maybe my father paid him to say that." These same kinds of reasons are used by insecure people today to ward off any compliments they hear about themselves. But word pictures have the ability to capture people's attention in spite of their defenses.

How do we know word pictures really got through to Solomon's bride in their marriage? Just look at how her attitude changed over the course of their married life.

During their courtship, she viewed their relationship with a certain insecurity and possessiveness. These feelings are evident in the way she talked about their relationship: "*My beloved is mine, and I am his*" (2:16, italics added).

As their story continues after the wedding—and as she grew more secure in his love—watch the subtle but powerful change in how she viewed their relationship. Once they were married, she told the ladies of the court, "*I am my beloved's, and my beloved is mine*" (6:3, italics added). This statement shows a little more security.

Then, as their story draws to a close, she even said, "*I am my beloved's, and his desire is toward me*" (7:10, italics added). This final statement shows a lot more security than her view of their relationship just before their wedding night.

Why? The major reason is the way word pictures of praise and great value have brought security to an insecure woman's heart. Repeatedly (more than fifty times), Solomon expressed his high value for his bride by using word pictures, and his words gradually transformed her view of herself and her relationship.

Most people will listen to a message more intently when it comes packaged in a word picture. That is one reason Jesus used word pictures to communicate both praise and condemnation through his teachings and his parables. He would talk about being the Good Shepherd who watched over the flock, the Bread of Life that would provide spiritual nourishment. By speaking in word pictures, he was able to penetrate the walls of insecurity and mistrust these people had put up, because stories and images hold a key to our hearts that simple words do not.

Jesus' extended object lessons kept his audience's attention even when some, like the Pharisees, did not really hear what he was saying. That is another advantage of word pictures. They are not just effective in getting through to an insecure person. They can also be immensely helpful in getting around the defenses of someone who for some reason just does not want to listen.

Gary once counseled a young couple who had been having heated arguments for a long period of time. Things had become so strained between Bill and Barb that they had even considered separating. They were angry and defensive when they walked into the office and they sat with their arms crossed, looking straight ahead. Their nonverbals were saying, "You just try and say something to change my mind. I'm walking out of this marriage."

Bill was a rugged outdoorsman who had moved his family outside the city limits so he would be close to the hunting and fishing he loved. He didn't mind the thirty-five-mile drive to work each day as long as he could live in the wilderness. At first, his wife had enjoyed joining him on his backpacking trips. But now she stayed home with their two young children, and he did all his camping alone.

Barb was a petite city girl who enjoyed socializing. With the move out of town, she was now an hour from her closest friend. The only socializing she did during the day was with two toddlers. While Barb loved her children deeply, being isolated from her friend and having a husband who hunted or fished every spare minute was leading her to become bitter and resentful.

After listening to Bill and Barb talk for more than an hour about how insensitive the other person was, Gary shared with them this word picture that opened their eyes to a completely new way of viewing each other.

"Let me close our time together by telling you two a word picture that came to my mind as I listened to you talk. Bill, I could see you as a picture, hanging on a wall, of a mighty stag with a huge rack of antlers. You are standing proudly near a mountain stream, looking over the forest, with your doe and newborn fawns in the background. The square frame around the picture is heavy and made out of antique wood.

"Barb, I see you as a painting of a delicate, beautiful wildflower with dazzling colors and fine brushstrokes. Your picture has a lovely oval mat, and the frame is narrow and classy looking, with white glossy paint.

"Both of you are beautiful pictures even though you look so different. However, you're not seeing the beauty in the other person's picture. In fact, each of you keeps trying to repaint the other picture to make it look more like your own. This week I'd like you to put down your brushes and look for the beauty that is already in the other person's painting. And let's get back together next week and talk about it."

What a difference a week can make. That one word picture communicated volumes to this couple. Instead of trying to change each other into their own image, they actually began appreciating each other—and rediscovering the attraction that had drawn them together in the first place. Instead of dishonoring each other in anger, they began to be more patient with each other and to honor the uniqueness of the person they married. All because a word picture managed to circumvent their defenses and speak to their hearts.

Key #4: Use Word Pictures to Point Out a Person's Potential

A fourth reason for using word pictures is to illustrate the undeveloped traits of a person—qualities they may not acknowledge or even be aware of. Jesus did this in changing Simon's name to Peter, which literally means "rock" in Greek. Peter certainly didn't act like a rock of strength and stability when he tried to talk Jesus out of going to the cross, when he went to sleep in the garden, or when he denied Jesus three times. But Jesus knew Peter's heart and understood what he could become. After the Resurrection, Peter did become the rock Jesus had pictured him to be.

In a modern-day instance, I saw this happen with a young lady in my home church. This young woman's husband had divorced her to pursue an immoral relationship. Left with two young children under three and no marketable skills or workforce experience, she faced one struggle after another. But six years after her husband left, she was back on her feet, with a good job that allowed her to spend time with her children and still provide for their basic financial needs.

When we asked her what had helped her most during those early, difficult years, she said, "The Lord was certainly the greatest source of help to us when Jack first left; but from a human perspective, I would have to point to my father. Every time I wanted to quit school or just give up, he would say to me, 'You'll make it, Jenny. You're my Rock of Gibraltar. I know you'll make it.' I didn't feel like a rock at the time. My whole world seemed to be caving in. But it helped me so much to know that he pictured me this way. It gave me the hope that maybe I could make it."

MULTIPLYING THE MESSAGE

To review, we have discovered four keys to using word pictures in communicating words of high value:

1. Use an everyday object.
2. Match the emotional meaning of the trait you are praising with the object you've picked.

3. Use word pictures to unravel defenses.
4. Use word pictures to point out a person's potential.

Here's one last example of how powerful a word picture can be in blessing a person. It's an example I look at every day.

One afternoon when our daughters were young, I took them outside to play. I was heading out of town the next day for a seminar, so I wanted us to have some time together before I left.

At one point, Laura (our youngest) walked up and handed me a clothespin. The metal was rusted and the wood, water-soaked and starting to splinter. I was looking at it when Cindy called us in to dinner.

As I walked inside, I stopped at the door and handed Cindy the clothespin.

"What's this?" she said.

"It's you," I said.

"Meaning . . . ?" Cindy said quizzically.

"Meaning . . . just pretend this is a solid-gold clothespin. Sweetheart, you do such a great job of holding everything together when I have to go on a trip. You're like a solid-gold clothespin."

Cindy smiled, we all trouped in to dinner, and I left on my trip the next morning. When I came home, I learned something dramatic had happened—to the clothespin, that is. Cindy had painted it white, drawn a small red heart on it, and glued a magnet to the back. Today, years later, it's still on our refrigerator, right where *really important* things go.

To everyone else, that painted clothespin may look like a cute knickknack from a craft store or even something one of the kids made. But to Cindy it says, "I'm a clothespin. I do a great job of holding everything together for my family."

A very well-known saying tells us that one picture is worth a thousand words. When we link a word picture with a message of high value, we multiply our message a thousand times. That is the amazing power of the third element of the blessing.

NINE

The Fourth Element:
Picturing a Special Future

"How could anyone as dumb and ugly as you have such a good-looking child?" Mark's mother was grinning as she cuddled her grandson in her arms. To most observers, her words might have been brushed aside as a bad joke, but they brought instant tears to Mark's eyes.

"Stop it!" Mark said emphatically. "That's all I've ever heard from you. It's taken me years to believe I'm not ugly and dumb. Why do you think I haven't been home in so long? I don't ever want you to call me dumb again."

Mark's mother sat in stunned silence. Tears came to her eyes. She really had meant her words as a joke. But for the first time one of her children had had the courage to confront her. For years, without realizing the impact of her words, this mother had constantly kidded her children about being stupid, fat, or ugly. After all, she had been kidded unmercifully by *her* mother when she was growing up . . .

What Kind of Future
Do Our Words Picture?

When it comes to predictions about their future, children are literalists—particularly when they hear predictions from their parents, the most important people (from an earthly perspective) in their lives. This is why communicating a special future to a child is such an important part of giving the family blessing. But this element of the blessing isn't just for children. Feeling and believing that the future is hopeful and something to look forward to can greatly affect anyone's attitude on life. By picturing a special future for our children, spouse, or friends, we are providing them with a clear light for their paths in life.

Have you ever been camping in the woods on a dark night? If you have, you probably remember what it's like to walk away from your campfire into the night. In only a few steps, darkness can seem to swallow you up. Turning around and walking back toward the fire is a great deal more reassuring than groping around in the dark. But if you light a lantern from that fire, you actually will be able to see your way on the dark path.

Words that picture a special future act like a campfire on a dark night. They can draw a person toward the warmth of genuine concern and fulfilled potential. They act like the lantern as well. Instead of leaving us to stumble into a dark unknown, they can illuminate a pathway lined with hope and purpose.

Children (and others) begin to take steps down the positive pathway pictured for them when they hear words like these: "God has given you such a sensitive heart. I wouldn't be surprised if you end up helping a great many people when you get older," or "You are such a good helper. When you grow up and marry someday, you're going to be such a help to your wife (or husband) and family."

Of course, the opposite is true as well. If children hear only words that predict relationship problems or personal inadequacies, they can turn and travel down the hurtful path that has been pictured for them. This can happen if they hear statements like "You'd better hope you can find someone who can take care of you when you're older. You're so irresponsible you'll never be able to do anything for yourself," or "Why bother to study so much? You'll just get married and drop out of school anyway."

Let's look back at Mark's family to see how this happened in his home. Over the years, Mark's mother had repeatedly given her children a negative picture of their future.

"Nobody's going to want to date a fat mess like you!" she would say with a resounding laugh—and her daughter would ache inside.

"You might as well drop geometry now; that's for smart kids," she would remark—and her youngest son would throw down his pencil and quit trying to understand the math problems in front of him, hating himself for giving up.

From the mother's conscious perspective, these were just playful words. But they failed to acknowledge the critical need every child has to have a special future pictured for him or her. The way Mark's mother talked to her children robbed them of a crucial part of the blessing. The prospect of facing the future as dumb, ugly, or unappealing—even if such words were spoken in jest—eroded each child's self-confidence, and the fallout was devastating.

For Mark's brother and sister, the mother's descriptions became self-fulfilling prophecies. The youngest son dropped out of high school after flunking his junior year. After all, he "never was intelligent" anyway. Mark's older sister neglected her appearance so much that no boys were interested in dating her. After all, she knew she was "ugly" anyway. Mark took just the opposite approach to the negative future pictured for him. He became the family overachiever. His entire lifestyle bordered on extreme workaholism—all in an attempt to try to prove to his mother that her predictions were wrong.

If you add up the incredible costs exacted from the children in this family, you can see how devastating picturing a negative future can be. You can also see why the blessing in the Scriptures puts such a high priority on picturing a special future for each child.

PICTURING A SPECIAL FUTURE IN PATRIARCHAL HOMES

In the Old Testament, picturing a special future for children was an important part of the formal family blessing. We can see this by looking at the words Isaac spoke to Jacob.

> *Therefore may God give you*
> *Of the dew of heaven,*
> *Of the fatness of the earth,*
> *And plenty of grain and wine.*
> *Let peoples serve you,*
> *And nations bow down to you.*
> *Be master over your brethren,*
> *And let your mother's sons bow down to you.*
> *Cursed be everyone who curses you,*
> *And blessed be those who bless you! (Gen. 27:28–29)*

When Isaac spoke these words, much of his son's blessing lay in the future. Jacob was not swamped with people wanting to bow down to him, and he had no land or flocks of his own that God could bless. Yet the picture gave him the security of knowing he had something to look forward to.

One generation later, Jacob's son Judah received a similar picture of a special future: "Judah, you are he whom your brothers shall praise; your hand shall be on the neck of your enemies; your father's children shall bow down before you" (Gen. 49:8). Like father, like son—Jacob passed down this part of the blessing. This blessing pictured a special future that would take years to become reality, but offered Judah a special hope as each year unfolded.

As we mentioned in chapter 5, these patriarchs' words had a prophetic nature that is not a part of the blessing today. We as parents cannot predict our children's futures with biblical accuracy, but we can provide them with the hope and direction that can lead to meaningful goals. As they begin to live up to these goals, they gain added security in an insecure world.

In Orthodox Jewish homes and services, the wish for a special future for each child is constantly present. At the synagogue, the rabbi often says to young boys, "May this little child grow to manhood. Even as he has entered onto the Covenant, so may he enter into the study of Torah, into the wedding-canopy and into a life of good deeds."[1] In the home, family blessings are also interlaced with words that picture a special future.

I saw this aspect of the blessing clearly in a Jewish home I was invited to visit one Thanksgiving. By the time I arrived, almost forty people were preparing or waiting patiently for a scrumptious dinner. Three generations—grandparents, parents, and their children—had assembled for this special occasion.

When the meal was prepared and before it could be served, the patriarch of the family (the grandfather) gathered all the family together. He had all the men and their sons stand on one side of the living room and all the women and their daughters stand on the other side. He then went around the room, placing his hands on the head of every person and speaking to them. To each man, he said, "May God richly bless you, and may he make thee as Ephraim and Manasseh." And each woman received the words, "May God richly bless you, and may you grow to be like Rebekah and Sarah."

From the oldest grown son to the youngest grandchild, this time of blessing pictured a special future for each person in the room—even me, a stranger to him. Far from being a meaningless ritual, it provided everyone with a warm wish for a fulfilling life in the years to come.

LIVING THE BLESSING

A Special Future . . . in Your Past

Think back over your childhood and write down some of the words that were often shared with you regarding your future. What did the important adults in your life predict about you? Why do you think they said what they said (pride, jealousy, denial, desire to hurt or bless, careful attention to your talents and gifts)? How have past words about who you are and what your future would be affected the way you live your life today? Have any become a reality? What would it take to reverse or overcome negative words that were communicated about you?

BRINGING OUT THE BEST IN THOSE WE BLESS

Picturing a special future for a child, spouse, or friend can help bring out the best in his or her life. It gives that person a positive direction to strive toward and surrounds him or her with hope. We can see this very thing in our relationship with the Lord. Listen to the beautiful way the prophet Jeremiah assures us of the special future we have in our relationship with him: "For I know the thoughts that I think toward you, says the LORD, thoughts of peace and not of evil, to give you a future and a hope" (29:11).

Jesus also went to great lengths to assure his insecure disciples that they had a special future with him. During their last Passover meal together, Jesus made sure they knew their future together would not end at his death. "In My Father's house are many mansions," he told them, "if it were not so, I would have told you. I go to prepare a place for you. And if I go and prepare a place for you, I will come again and receive you to Myself; that where I am, there you may be also" (John 14:2–3).

Time and time again in the Bible, God gives us a picture of our special future with him. However, his written Word is not the only way God communicates this message to us. Scattered throughout nature are a number of physical pictures of spiritual truths, pictures that illustrate the importance of providing a special future for the ones we love.

Anyone who has ever watched a caterpillar emerge from its cocoon as a butterfly has seen such a picture. The cater-pillar is probably not on anyone's list of the world's "ten most beautiful creatures." Yet a caterpillar has the potential to be transformed into a list-topping, beautiful butterfly. What does this have to do with the blessing? Words that picture a special future for a child, spouse, or friend can act as agents of this kind of transformation in that individual's life.

Words really do have that kind of transforming power. The apostle Paul certainly thought so.

The actual term for the transformation of a caterpillar to a butterfly is *metamorphosis*, based on a Greek word. Paul used this same Greek word in the book of Romans. He was aware that the world had tremendous power to squeeze and mold the saints in Rome into a godless image. To counter this, he told these young believers, "Be transformed by the renewing of your mind, that you may prove what is that good and acceptable and perfect will of God" (Rom. 12:2).

What does it mean to be "transformed by the renewing of your mind"? One excellent New Testament commentator explains the concept this way: "Since men are transformed by the action of the mind, transformed by what they think, how important to have the organ of thought renewed!"[2] In other words, godly thoughts and thinking patterns have the ability to transform us into godly men or women rather than leaving us to be squeezed into the imperfect mold of the world. Let's see how this works with regard to the blessing.

Children are filled with the potential to be all God intended them to be. It is as if the Lord places them on our doorstep one day, and we as parents are left as stewards of their abilities. During the years we have children in our homes, the words we speak to them can wrap around them like a cocoon. What we say can shape and develop them in a positive way.

In chapter 8, we saw how this picture of the future helped a child named Diane. In spite of her physical handicap, Diane's parents provided emotional support and words of a special future that lay before her. When Diane emerged from the cocoon of her parents' home and went out into the world, her love for the Lord and other people shone as brightly as the colors on a monarch butterfly's wings.

Sadly, it does not always happen that way. In some homes the words that wrap around developing children actually restrict growth and positive change rather than promote it. This restriction was true in Barry's home.

"You're a bum. You'll always be a bum." Barry's father said these words to him on his way to his college graduation— a ceremony his father did not even attend. This was not the first time, nor would it be the last, that Barry would hear these words. In fact, they were the only comments Barry ever received from his father about his future.

When I saw Barry in counseling, he had just lost an important position in a major insurance company. At first glance, this seemed hard to believe. Barry was extremely intelligent and gifted. He was an eloquent speaker, with that charisma that marks many successful businessmen. However, less than a year after landing his current position, Barry had self-destructed. All the motivation he had shown when seeking the job seemed to evaporate once he was hired. He became irresponsible in handling projects and people, and within six months he was looking for work.

What was it that acted like an anchor in holding Barry back from reaching his God-given potential? Three words: "You're a bum." Repeated over and over in Barry's presence and in his mind—even eight years after his father's death— they had wrapped themselves around him like a restricting cocoon, and he emerged an insecure, irresponsible, defeated, and self-defeating man.

A law of physics says that water cannot rise above its source. A similar principle could be applied to Barry and many people like him. If a parent pictures for a child that his or her value in life is low, that child will find it difficult to rise above these words. One insightful study of fathers and their daughters revealed a direct relationship between the life achievements of the women studied and the level of their father's acceptance of them.[3] Our experience as counselors indicate the same is true for boys. Those who truly desire to give their children the blessing will provide room for them to grow by encouraging their potential and by picturing a special future for them.

Let's look at another important picture in nature that mirrors what happens when we bless our children with words of a special future. This picture, explained to me by my twin brother, Jeff, a cancer doctor, is found in something that happens in every cell in our bodies.[4]

Imagine a typical cell in your body by thinking of a circle. Attached to the outside of this circle are a number of receptor points. We could picture these receptor points as little squares that almost look like gears on a wheel. To make things easier for us to understand, let's picture these receptor sites as little square people.

Floating around near the cell are hormones and enzymes. Think of them as Harry Hormone and Ethyl Enzyme, who would each love to shake hands with (or activate) these little receptor people. And while a great number of these hormones and enzymes have the ability to connect with a receptor site, some have a special ability to stimulate a cell's activity and cause it to work harder.

We can picture this special ability as someone coming up to you and shaking your hand up and down so vigorously that your whole body shakes and you feel energized. In fact, your neighbors start shaking and feel energized too. Such stimulation by hormones and enzymes, which causes the receptor sites to work harder, is called *positive cooperativity*.

But other hormones and enzymes act in a negative way when they shake hands with a receptor site. This is negative cooperativity. Have you ever had your hand squeezed so hard that you almost crumpled over in pain? That's the kind of thing that happens when these hormones and enzymes grab hold of a receptor site. In fact, not only does this one receptor site shut down and stop working because its "hand" is being squeezed, but all the receptor sites around it stop too.

And this applies to the blessing . . . how?

Words that picture a special future for a child act like positive hormones that attach themselves to a cell. They stimulate all kinds of positive feelings and decisions within a child that can help him or her grow and develop. Words of a special future can inspire a child to work on a particular talent, have the confidence to try out for a school office, or even share his or her faith with other children.

But just like the negative hormones that shut down cell activity, a critical, negative picture of the future can crush or pinch off healthy growth in a child. Emotional, physical, and even spiritual growth in a child can be stunted because of the stifling effect of a negative picture of the future.

THE POWER OF PAST CONSISTENCY

By now you *know* how important it is to provide our children with words that point out a special future for them. But words alone may not be enough to get this message across to those we want to bless. Unless our words of a special future are backed up by a consistent track record, the person we are trying to bless may be unwilling or unable to believe what we say.

If we are serious about offering a message of a special future to our children, we need to follow the example the Lord sets. His consistency in the past acts as a solid footing on which words of a special future can stand.

Throughout the Scriptures the basis for believing God's Word in the future lies in his consistency in fulfilling his

Word in the past. In Psalm 105:5 we read, "Remember His marvelous works which he has done, His wonders, and the judgments of His mouth." And in Psalm 33:9 the psalmist wrote, "He spoke, and it was done; He commanded, and it stood fast."

Because God has been reliable in the past, his words of a special future for us in the present have credence. The same principle applies to our desire to picture a special future for those we wish to bless. Our credibility in the past—or lack of it—will directly affect how our words are received in the present. Just as it did for Ted.

Ted was a sales manager for a national marketing chain. His job responsibilities meant that he was in town one week and out the next. In an average year (adding in an occasional back-to-back trip and sales conferences and subtracting major holidays), Ted was gone thirty-one weeks a year. His schedule ate away at the credibility of his statements that his children had a special future.

Ted had two young children at home, and they loved their daddy dearly. All week they would besiege their mother with the question, "Is Daddy coming home today?" When Daddy finally did come home, however, he was so tired from jet lag and his demanding schedule that he had little energy to spend meaningful time with the children.

Ted did a good job of "picturing" a special future for his children. The only problem was that he never followed through on his word. For instance, he would notice his daughter's deep love for animals and tell her, "Samantha, we're going to get a horse for you so you can ride it and take care of it. You might even become a veterinarian someday." To his son, who was very athletic for his age, he would say, "Bobby, you're pro shortstop material. Just give me a little time to rest up; then we'll go down to the park, and I'll hit you some grounders." But in just a few days it would be time for Ted to go back on the road. And somehow there was never enough time to settle all the details of buying a horse for Sam, never a free afternoon to hit grounders to Bobby.

After nine years of being on the road, Ted finally realized that he needed to greatly reduce his traveling schedule if he was ever going to build a secure marriage and family life. He even took a cut in pay to take a position that would enable him to stay at home. One of the first things he did was to surprise his daughter with a new horse—only now, Samantha wasn't interested in horses anymore. Neither was Bobby interested in going with his father to a pro baseball game. His children had listened to the empty promise of a special future for them for so long that Ted's words carried as much weight as the air used to speak them. They had their friends, their relationship with their mother, a new set of interests, and a deep-set impression that any future they had would not include their father's involvement.

This story has a happy ending, however. Ted truly loved his wife and children, and he persevered in trying to regain the lost ground with his family. As the weeks turned into months, Ted began to build up a track record of honored commitments. It took nearly two years, but he finally built up a *past* with his children that assured them he really did want the best for their futures. Interestingly, Samantha even began to rekindle an interest in animals, and Bobby dug his baseball glove out of the bottom of the closet.

Perhaps your past has been anything but consistent with those you want to bless. Today really *is* the first day of the rest of your life. And by honoring commitments to your children today, you can begin to build the kind of history that words of a special future need to rest on. Remember, there is no such thing as "quality time" that makes up for inconsistency in our relationships. We need to have a track record of daily decisions that demonstrate our commitment to our children, our spouses, or anyone we would bless. Only then will our words of a special future really find their mark.

THE POWER OF PRESENT COMMITMENT

As we have mentioned, if our words of a special future are to take hold and grow, we need to demonstrate commitment in the present. This idea of commitment is so important that we will spend the next chapter examining it in depth. However, one aspect of a present commitment applies directly to picturing a special future. The effectiveness of our predictions depends on the degree of certainty our children have that we will be around long enough to see those predictions come to pass.

Gary's oldest child, Kari (now a mother herself), brought up this subject at the dinner table when she was in grade school.

"We were all sitting around the table, enjoying a meal my wife, Norma, had prepared. We were all talking about our day and having a nice conversation when, out of the blue, Kari turned to her mother and said, 'Mom, do you think you'll ever divorce Dad?' Everyone got quiet the moment she asked the question, and Norma nearly choked on her dinner. 'Kari!' she said in shock. 'You know that I would never divorce your dad.' Then stopping to think about it a little more, Norma added with a twinkle in her eye, 'Murder, maybe, but never divorce!' After we stopped laughing, we found out why Kari had asked her question. We were only two months into the school year, and already the parents of two of her classmates had gotten a divorce."

What Gary's daughter was asking that night was the same thing every child asks about his or her parents—whether out loud or in the silence of his or her heart: "Will you be here in the future as I grow up, or will one of you leave me?"

Recently I counseled a husband and wife who were constantly fighting. I had asked the entire family to come in to try to get a better picture of what was happening with the couple. That meant that I had an eleven-year-old boy and a six-year-old girl join us for our counseling session. I began the session by addressing the six-year-old young lady. (Children are *soooooo* honest, even when their parents hesitate to be too specific.)

"What bothers you the most about your parents' arguing?" I asked. Her answer surprised me. What was causing her the greatest pain and insecurity wasn't their loud voices or even what they said. It was this: "Every time my daddy gets mad at my mom, he takes off his wedding ring and throws it away."

Children are incredibly perceptive, and this little girl was no exception. While her father said it was "no big deal," his habit of pulling his wedding ring off his finger and throwing it somewhere in the house sent out a message loud and clear. Every time he "threw away" his wedding ring, this little girl saw her future with her parents (the greatest source of security a child has) go sailing right along with it.

Words of a special future for a child can dissolve into ashes when a husband or wife walks out on a relationship. In a later chapter, we will see just how difficult it is for some children who have lost a parent due to divorce or death to feel blessed (and also how a single parent can help correct this). For those of you who are married, an important part of picturing a special future for your children is keeping your present commitment to your spouse strong and intact.

LIVING THE BLESSING

A Special Future for Someone You Love

Think about a person you love and want to bless—such as your child. List some of the qualities you see in that person that, if developed, could cause him or her to blossom in the future. How can you most effectively (using word pictures) express that possibility as part of your blessing? What have you done or said so far to help that person envision a special future? In what ways do you undermine your own words by failing to follow through or show commitment? Are there people in your life for which you have a hard time envisioning a special future? If so, why do you think that is—and how can you move past it?

A GUIDING LIGHT TO FOLLOW

Thankfully, many people realize the importance of providing their children, spouses, or friends with a picture of a special future. These people use words of blessing to help mold, shape, and guide a person to move into the rich future God has in store for him or her. Even when that person is someone like Marcia.

Marcia struggled throughout her years in school. If it took her classmates a half hour to do an assignment, you can bet Marcia would only be halfway through the same project an hour later. Her parents even received the disturbing news from her teacher that Marcia was being placed in the "slow learners" group. But this news did not discourage Marcia's parents from picturing a special future for her. While they knew she was struggling in school, they also knew their daughter had many positive characteristics.

Rather than pushing Marcia to "hurry up" or work faster, her parents would praise her for being methodical and for staying with an assignment until she finished it. They also noticed that Marcia had an obvious gift for verbally encouraging her younger sisters and the neighbor children and for explaining things to them in a way they could understand. They began to encourage her to use these talents by letting her help them teach the young children in Sunday school and use her gifts in serving these little ones.

After Sunday school one morning Marcia announced to her parents that she wanted to be a teacher when she grew up. Her comments could have been met with a chuckle, a "What'll you want to be next week?" or even the pious words, "Now, Marcia, let's be realistic." (The quarter's grades had just come out, and Marcia was still at the bottom of her class.)

However, Marcia's parents looked beyond her sagging test scores and recognized her God-given talents. Instead of laughing at her, they pointed out these gifts and encouraged her. They said that if she was willing to stay with it, one day she would become a teacher—a future that few "slow learners" would ever dream of picturing for themselves or hear pictured for them by their parents.

Marcia continued to struggle through every year of school. Her parents had to pay for tutors in grade school and special reading classes in high school. When Marcia decided to go to college, it took her six and a half years to graduate from a four-year program because she could not handle taking a full load of classes. Nonetheless, on a beautiful Saturday afternoon in May, Marcia graduated from college with an elementary education teaching degree.

While graduation day meant that many of her classmates were just beginning to look for a job, Marcia already had one.

She had done such a magnificent job of student teaching at an elementary school in a fine school district that the principal had asked her to return the next year and take over a first grade teaching position.

Actually, three people deserved to be honored that graduation day. Marcia certainly deserved a great deal of credit for plodding forward day by day to reach her goal of being an elementary school teacher. Yet her parents also deserved high praise for encouraging her to reach her dream. Even more, they deserved acclaim for encouraging their daughter's dream by picturing a special future for her—even when years' worth of school report cards had branded Marcia a "slow learner."

Are you providing your children, spouse, or intimate friends with a blessing that pictures a special future for them? Did your parents take the time and effort to provide you with the hope of a bright tomorrow as you grew up? Wherever the blessing is given or received, words that picture a special future are always shared—words that represent the fourth element of the blessing.

TEN

The Fifth Element:
An Active Commitment

MOST CHILDREN HAVE at least one subject in school that they particularly dread. Whether it is history, English, or geography, that course represents the worst hour of the school day. For Gary, that subject was geometry. Yet it was a geometry class in high school that taught him the incredible power of an active commitment—the fifth element of the blessing.

"Mathematics was always the subject I dreaded the most. In grade school it was my poorest subject, and that continued to be true during my first two years of high school. In fact, when I had to repeat geometry my senior year, I was sure after only a month that I was going to flunk the course. My only solace was the fact that more than half the class was flunking with me. Our teacher would constantly remind us of this fact by arranging our chairs according to our current grade. Those of us who were failing lined the back wall.

"One Monday morning, when we dragged ourselves into

the classroom, all that changed. Sitting behind the teacher's desk was a substitute teacher—good news in itself. Then, when we found out that our regular teacher had been reassigned to a different district, we felt like the people in Paris during World War II who had just been liberated! But the fact remained that half of us were still failing the course. And I was still discouraged because I believed I was below average when it came to mathematics.

"Then the new teacher said something that literally changed my life. In fact, it motivated me so much that I ended up minoring in mathematics in college. While I didn't realize it at the time, he actually blessed me and the other students in the class. He did this by providing us with a clear picture of an active commitment—the fifth element of the blessing.

"Standing before the class that morning, our new teacher told us, 'If anyone fails this class, then I have failed.' He made a commitment that morning to do whatever it took to see that we all passed the course. He pledged himself to see that we learned and enjoyed the subject to the best of our abilities. Whether that meant his staying after school to tutor us or even coming in for a special session on the weekend, he dedicated himself to see that each of us made it through the course. Nearly every Saturday morning he would help several of us with our homework, then play a little volleyball with us for fun.

"Imagine the turnaround that took place in that class. Where once we had dreaded geometry, now it became something we looked forward to. Even better was what happened the last day of school, when our teacher posted our grades. We all passed, and I received my first A in math!

"You should have seen it. We were all jumping around and hugging each other. All because one man committed himself to a struggling bunch of students."

In the school of life, children desperately need adults—preferably parents—who will make the same type of active commitment that teacher did to Gary. In the areas where they are weak, they need to be encouraged and built up. They need to be appropriately touched or hugged and verbally praised for their strengths. When they are hurting, they need to feel someone's arms around them, giving them assurance and helping them back on their feet. Undeveloped potential needs to be brought out into the open and developed. These actions and attitudes are a part of bestowing the blessing. And all of them need to be given not just once, but again and again. Which brings us to the fifth element of the blessing.

MAKING THE BLESSING HAPPEN

In the past several chapters we have looked at the first four elements of the blessing:

- Meaningful touch
- A spoken (or written) message
- Attaching high value
- Picturing a special future

These four elements are the building blocks of the blessing. But the mortar that holds them together is an active commitment, the fifth element of the blessing.

Why is an active commitment such an important part of the blessing? As we have seen in earlier chapters, words of blessing alone are not enough. They need to be backed by an ongoing dedication to see the blessing come to pass.

This principle is what the apostle James wants us to

understand in his letter. There we read, "If a brother or sister is naked and destitute of daily food, and one of you says to them, 'Depart in peace, be warmed and filled,' but you do not give them the things which are needed for the body, what does it profit?" (James 2:15–16).

To answer the apostle's question, words without commitment are about as useful as a crooked politician's promises on the eve of Election Day. Giving the blessing involves action, linked to our words. If we *talk the talk* but then fail to put the elements of the blessing into practice, we leave our children, spouse, and friends undernourished and ill-clothed in their need for love and acceptance.

LIVING THE BLESSING

An Active Commitment and You

How dependable were the adults in your life when you were a child? Did any events (a death in the family, a divorce, a job issue) cause a parent or guardian to be very busy, distracted, or absent at certain times? Write down what you can remember about those times and how they affected you. Did you feel that the adults in your life had your best interests at heart? Did anyone make an effort to understand what was going on with you? Looking back, do you think you were disciplined appropriately? How has the style of discipline you experienced as a child affected the way you think and act today?

The blessing as found in Scripture offers a strong contrast to speaking empty words to our loved ones. It features several important steps we can take to demonstrate an active commitment to those we want to bless.

Step #1: Ask the Lord to Confirm the Blessing

When you look at the blessing in the Old Testament, something that stands out is the way the patriarchs committed their children to the Lord. When Isaac blessed Jacob, we read, "May *God* give you of the dew of heaven, of the fatness of the earth" (Gen. 27:28, italics added). Years later, when Jacob blessed his sons and grandchildren, he began by saying, "The *God* who has been my shepherd all my life to this day . . . bless the lads" (Gen. 48:15–16 NASB, italics added).

One reason these patriarchs called on God to confirm their child's blessing was because they were sure of his commitment to them. We can see this clearly with Isaac and Jacob.

In Genesis 26, Isaac was facing real problems. Living in the desert, he knew that his most precious assets were the wells he dug for fresh water. Twice Isaac had been driven from wells his father had dug. He was then forced to dig a third well to provide water for his flocks and his family. That night, as if to assure Isaac of his future in this land, "the LORD appeared to him . . . and said, 'I am the *God* of your father Abraham; do not fear, for I am with you. I will bless you and multiply your descendants'" (Gen. 26:24, italics added).

Isaac had been driven away from two wells that rightfully belonged to him. Hearing his heavenly Father declare his ongoing commitment to Isaac's family must have been like drinking cool, refreshing water on a hot summer's day.

God echoed those words of commitment to Jacob at a difficult time in his own life. Fleeing his brother Esau's anger, Jacob stopped one night to sleep out in the desert. It was there that God spoke to him and said, "I am the LORD God of Abraham your father and the God of Isaac. . . . Behold, I am with you and will keep you wherever you go, and will bring you back to this land; for I will not leave you until I have done what I have spoken to you" (Gen. 28:13, 15).

Isaac and Jacob were sure of their relationships with God. A natural extension of that certainty was to ask the Lord to bless their children through them. This is something we frequently see in churches today.

This past Sunday, in churches all across the country, pastors closed their services with the words "May the Lord bless you, and keep you." By linking God's name to the blessing they spoke, these pastors were asking God himself to be the one to confirm it with his power and might—the very thing Isaac and Jacob did with their children.

We see the same idea in the dedication of children at a church. Often the pastor will lay his hands on children and say similar words of blessing, picturing the desire the parents and the entire congregation have in asking God to bless these little ones.

Wise parents will follow this practice in bestowing the blessing on their children. When they say, "May the Lord bless you," they are first recognizing and acknowledging that any strength they have to bestow the blessing comes from an all-powerful God. Even the very breath of life they have to speak words of blessing comes from him.

We are all prone to be inconsistent, and we stumble occasionally in providing the elements of the blessing for our children. In contrast, God remains changeless in his ability to give us strength to love our spouses and children the way we should.

A second important reason to commit our children to the Lord when we bless them is that doing so teaches them that God is personally concerned with their lives and welfare. Stressing that the Lord is interested in their being blessed is like introducing them to someone who can be their best friend, a personal encourager they can draw close to throughout their lives.

Bringing the Lord into our words of blessing provides a sense of security for a child that we as frail humans cannot convey. We saw this in the way the children in one family reacted after the unexpected death of their father.

Lindsay and Kelly were still in grade school when their father died of a massive heart attack at the age of forty-one. These children no longer had his arms to comfort them or his encouraging words to bless them. But they did have a certain knowledge that Papa was with the Lord and that Jesus would confirm their blessing. Why such certainty? Because a wise father and mother had reassured them of this fact over and over. Listen to the words of his widow, Lisa, who also drew comfort from her husband's words.

"Before Ray died, he used to gather us all together right before dinner. We would all get in a little circle, holding each other's hands. Then Papa would pray and thank the Lord for our day and for the food. He would end each prayer by squeezing my hand and saying, 'Lord Jesus, thank you that you are Lindsay's, and Kelly's, and Lisa's, and my Shepherd. Thank you that you will never leave us or forsake us. Amen.' It's been rough this past year without Ray, but it has helped so much to be able to remind the children that Jesus is still their Shepherd as well as their father's."

Children need the certainty and security that comes from our committing them and their blessing to the Lord. That does not mean that we do not participate in the blessing. Rather, it means that we recognize and acknowledge that only by God's strength and might will we ever be able to sustain our commitment to truly bless our children.

Step #2: Seek the Best Interests of the One Being Blessed

How do we begin committing ourselves to our children's best interests? First, as we have noted throughout the book, we must dedicate our time, energy, and resources to caring for them and spending time with them. However, Jacob observed another important principle in blessing his children. He recognized that every one of his children was unique.

In Genesis 48 and 49, Jacob (now called Israel) pronounced a blessing for each of his twelve sons and two of his grandchildren. After he had finished blessing each child, we read, "This is what their father [Jacob] said to them when he blessed them. He blessed them, *every one* with the blessing appropriate to him" (Gen. 49:28 NASB, italics added).

In Hebrew, the end of this very verse reads, "He blessed them, every one with his own blessing." While the elements of the blessing might remain the same, how they are applied in blessing a child is an individual concern. One daughter might need a dozen hugs and kisses at night before going to bed while her sister does well with two. One son might feel secure with hearing encouraging words only once while his brother may need to hear "You can do it" over and over again in approaching the same activity. Wise parents will realize that each child has his or her own unique set of needs. The book of Proverbs shows us this.

Most of us are familiar with the verse, "Train up a child in the way he should go, and when he is old he will not depart from it" (Prov. 22:6). However, another helpful way to view this verse would be to translate it, "Train up a child according to his bent . . ."[1] In training (or blessing) a child, we need to take a personal interest in each child. The better we know our children and their unique set of needs, the better we will be able to give them their own unique blessing.

Please pay close attention to this next statement: physical proximity does not equal personal knowledge. We can spend years under the same roof with our spouses and children and still be intimate strangers. Many people feel as though they know another person's interests and opinions because they took an active interest in their lives in the past. However, people's thoughts, dreams, and desires can change over the years. Doctors tell us that every cell in our body wears out and is replaced by new cells within a few years. We are constantly changing both physically and emotionally.

In our homes we can be people who are close in terms of proximity to each other but far away in terms of understanding the other person's real desires, needs, goals, hopes, and fears. However, we can combat this distance by taking the time to observe and understand the unique aspects of those we wish to bless.

Blessing our children involves understanding their unique bents. In addition, it means being willing to do what is best for those children, even if it means having to correct them when they are wrong.

Step #3: Discipline When Appropriate

Discipline may seem the very opposite of blessing another person. But in actuality we bless our children by providing them with the appropriate discipline. We see this when we look back at the individual blessings Jacob gave to each of his children.

Genesis 49 records a blessing for each son. We are told this very clearly in verse 28: "He [Jacob] blessed them, every one with the blessing appropriate to him" (NASB). However, at first glance the blessing that Reuben, the oldest son, received looks more like a curse than a blessing. However, Jacob dealt with each son individually, and in Reuben's case his blessing included discipline as well as praise:

> *Reuben, you are my firstborn,*
> *My might and the beginning of my strength,*
> *The excellency of dignity and the excellency of power.*
> *Unstable as water, you shall not excel,*
> *Because you went up to your father's bed;*
> *Then you defiled it. (Gen. 49:3–4)*

If we look closely at these verses, Jacob balances words of praise with words of correction. Reuben had several positive qualities his father praised (his might, strength, dignity, and power). However, he also had a glaring lack of discipline in his life. His unbridled passions had led him to the bed of one of his father's concubines. As a result he now was being disciplined for his actions.

It should not surprise us that blessing and discipline go hand in hand. If we genuinely love someone, we will not allow that person to stray into sin or be hurt in some way without trying to correct him or her. This lesson is explained by the writer of Hebrews when he says, "MY SON, DO NOT REGARD LIGHTLY THE DISCIPLINE OF THE LORD . . . FOR THOSE WHOM THE LORD LOVES HE DISCIPLINES" (12:5–6 NASB).

God actively deals with our wrong behavior rather than merely ignoring it because he sees us as his beloved children. Parents are naturally more concerned about the behavior of their own offspring than they are about other people's children. Like a loving parent with a highly valued child, God does care about our behavior.

Our sons' and daughters' actions should also concern us

if we are going to be a person who truly blesses them. We should not shy away from including loving discipline when it is appropriate and in their best interests.[2]

Initially, discipline can seem painful for both parents and children. Yet being willing to take that risk can help bring out the best in the children's lives by training them and guiding them to a place of peace and righteousness (Heb. 12:11). Discipline is an important way of actively committing ourselves to a child's best interest.

We have looked at three ways in which we can demonstrate an active commitment in blessing others: we can commit them to the Lord, we can seek their best interests, and we can apply appropriate discipline. A fourth way to show an active commitment is something I have seen modeled before me all my life.

Step #4: Becoming a Student of Those You Wish to Bless

Have you ever lost a loved one and then had to go in and pack up that person's personal possessions for an estate sale or to donate? For years my precious mother had her nest in a modest condominium in Phoenix, Arizona. It was a small place, easy for her to get around in after seven major operations due to rheumatoid arthritis slowing her down a bit. Yet it always seemed warm and welcoming, just like she was. All her life, my mother was busy, engaged in helping others, loving beyond words. She was lots of fun to be with and, as she grew older, to visit.

If you had dropped in to Mom's little condo during her last years, you would have seen something in her home that pictured what it means to be a student of your children. It probably wouldn't have caught your eye right off, though whenever I walked into my mother's home, it flashed at me like a neon light. It was also the thing that was the hardest for me to pack up after she passed away.

It was just a nondescript bookshelf. But it carried extra-special meaning for my two brothers and me.

One rack of the bookshelf was always filled with theology and psychology books. A second shelf overflowed with medical journals and books on genetics. The third shelf seemed even more out of place for a seventy-six-year-old arthritic woman. Lining this shelf were dozens of issues of *Heavy Equipment Digest* and how-to books on driving heavy equipment.

These seemingly unrelated books and magazines might lead a person to think this woman was an eccentric who would read anything or perhaps even had a touch of schizophrenia that caused her to jump from one topic to the next. Neither of these explanations would be close to the truth. This collection was actually a beautiful picture of the active commitment our mother made in choosing to give her sons the blessing.

Over the years my mother collected not only the books I had written but also the books on counseling and theology I had recommended to her. They were in her bookcase because she had taken an interest in my interests.

My twin brother, Jeff, is a cancer doctor who specializes in genetic research. To be able to understand his field of interest and converse with him about it, she read (or tried to read) loads of his medical and genetics articles and books. She even enrolled in a genetics class at the University of Arizona at the age of sixty so she could talk to Jeff about what was important to him. To be truthful, she ended up dropping the course after failing the first two major exams. However, sitting proudly on the shelf with the other highly technical books is the slightly worn textbook she struggled to understand. Each book is a trophy of her willingness to learn and her desire to communicate with my brother in his areas of interest.

But what about the magazines and books on operating road-construction equipment? My older brother, Joe, for years has been a heavy-equipment operator. Because my mother was committed to affirming and being a student of each son, she made a point of learning about his interests too. When she passed away at age seventy-six, she was a current subscriber to *Heavy Equipment Digest* and able to talk to Joe about the latest bulldozer or earth mover.

I doubt if *Heavy Equipment Digest* magazine receives many subscriptions from gray-haired, arthritic grandmothers, but they did from this one. All because she made a commitment to becoming a student of each son and his individual interests.

First Steps Toward Becoming a Student of Your Children

One thing that can greatly help us learn to become students of our children is to be lovingly persistent in communicating with them. Particularly if we have struggled in our relationships with our children or we haven't been close to them in the past, getting them to open up with us can take loving persistence. That doesn't mean badgering them or trying to pry the words out of their mouths. But it does mean consistently setting up times with them when meaningful communication can develop.

Second, realize that any shared activity with a child—from driving them to school or athletic practice to an airplane trip before they put on their headphones—offers tremendous opportunities to learn about our children.

And taking the initiative in asking questions can be a third important way to become students of our children. The Ask Your Children sidebar suggests just a few possible questions you can ask in those unguarded times at the hamburger place, at the ball game, or while taking a walk. Don't grill your child with questions as if you were giving a test. Just ask some casual questions in an offhanded way, and then really listen to the answers.

LIVING THE BLESSING

Ask Your Children

1. What do you daydream about most often?
2. What would you really enjoy doing when you are a young adult (twenty to thirty)?
3. Of all the people you have studied in the Bible, who would you most like to be like? Why?
4. What do you believe God wants you to do for humankind?
5. What type of boyfriend or girlfriend are you most attracted to, and why?
6. What is the best part of your school day? What is the worst?

Listening with full attention—that is the fourth practical way to get started in becoming a student of those we wish to bless. We actually bless our children by being emotionally present when they talk to us rather than being preoccupied with something else.

Have you ever carried on an entire conversation with a child while absorbed in a television show or reading Facebook posts? "Uh-huh" or "That sounds good, honey" uttered with our eyes glued to a screen does not communicate acceptance to our children, nor does it help us become a student of what they want to share.

One way to remind ourselves to actively listen to our children, spouses, or others is found in the book of Proverbs: "Bright eyes gladden the heart" (15:30 NASB).

My mother was so good at this, saying, "John, look at me," when she spoke to me about something important. Most of us have had the experience of walking into a room and seeing somebody's eyes "light up" when he or she saw us. That sparkle in another person's eyes communicates to us that the person is really interested in us and in what we have to say.

I once read of an interesting research study based on this very verse. A number of college men were given ten pictures of college-aged women who were more or less equally attractive. Each student was then asked to rate the pictures from "most attractive" to "least attractive."

What these young men did not know was that five of the women had been given an eye-drop solution just before their pictures were taken. This solution dilated the pupils in their eyes—the same thing that happens naturally when we are really glad to see someone. The results of the study were just as we might expect. The girls with the "bright eyes" were chosen hands down as the five most attractive women in the pictures.

Do our eyes *light up* when we listen to those we wish to bless? Our children or spouses will notice if they do or don't. We can decide to put down the iPhone or turn off the television to talk to our loved ones as we take an active interest in their interests. Active listening is an important part of communicating acceptance and blessing.

Those of us who are parents need to realize that our children are incredibly complicated people. So are our wives or husbands and friends. If we would begin today to list all their wishes, opinions, goals, and dreams, it would take us a life-time to complete the task. That is just the right amount of time needed to finish the course entitled "Becoming a Student of Your Loved Ones," a class men and women will enroll in if they are serious about bestowing an appropriate blessing to each person in their lives. All it takes to register is a decision to actively commit ourselves to others—and a pair of "bright eyes."

 If you are serious about commitment and accountability, go to TheBlessing.com and look for the link to a book called *HeartShift: The Two-Degree Difference.* You will be introduced to how powerful small changes—what I call "two-degree changes"—can be in helping you stay connected and committed to your children and spouse. TheBlessing.com even offers automated goal metrics—fancy words for a way to set and track your goals for blessing your family.

A KEY TO CONTINUED COMMITMENT

Many of us have shelves of notebooks from various marriage or parenting seminars and pages of notes from the pastor's sermons. Typically, we will get excited about a certain principle we have read or listened to. It may even make a dramatic difference in our lives—for a little while. However, let a few weeks go by, and that book usually finds its way to a dusty bookshelf with the other inspirational material, and the idea we were so excited about is more or less forgotten.

We have seen this so often in teaching people about blessing their children. At first we will see dramatic changes in their lives as they come to grips with whether they ever received the blessing themselves and how well they are doing in providing it for their children. We hope that has happened to you—that what you have read so far has helped you see your own life in a new and challenging light. Yet like any other call to commitment, the inner voice that encourages us to bless our children can get harder to hear as time wears on.

How can we establish a pattern of commitment that makes each element of the blessing a permanent resident in our homes? The best answer we know of is found in a single word: *accountability.*

For some reason we don't fully understand, genuine commitment to provide the blessing for our loved ones seems to grow best in small groups. When six to eight people take the time, week by week, to go through a book or a DVD series together, lasting changes are more likely to take place.

Imagine someone asking you how you did in terms of providing meaningful touch for your spouse or children that week, what encouraging words you spoke that attached high value to a son or daughter, or even, on a one-to-ten scale, how high your commitment to bless your family was that week?

Even better, imagine a place where you can admit your struggles and learn from other people's experiences (and mistakes). Does this description sound challenging and inspiring? It can happen during Sunday school at your church or in your home on a weeknight. All it takes is courage to ask honest questions and a loving spirit to share God's truth along with your own personal insights.

And you need one more thing: the nerve to pick up the phone and call those other people. A small group could consist of three or four couples who are in similar points of life. But it could also include single parents, grandparents, teachers, friends—anyone who is interested in enriching relationships and giving the blessing to those who need it. We suggest you consult your pastor or church leader and also pray about who might be good to ask.

Even if a small group does not seem feasible at the moment, you can still find sources of accountability. Why not stop right now and ask your spouse or a close friend how well you are doing in being a source of blessing to him or her. If your children are old enough, you can even ask them how they think you are doing. Children will usually be honest with you, and you can learn valuable lessons from them—if you will take the time to talk and listen to them.

LIVING THE BLESSING

Living Out an Active Commitment

As you read about this final element of the blessing, write out what you do on a regular basis to demonstrate your interest in and commitment to your child. What has this commitment cost you in terms of time, energy, or money? What issues in your life right now (long hours, marital struggle, depression, general business, lack of custody in a divorce) might be getting in the way? What actions could you take in the next three months to keep these issues from hindering your blessing? Make a list of possible sources of accountability for you in this area.

We know that asking questions—and, even more, being willing to answer them—can be threatening to some people. Even so, small groups or one-on-one conversations are a tremendous way to evaluate where we are at the present. These meetings also give us an added incentive to work on an area we are struggling with. Left on our own, most of us will tend to forget or sidestep these important areas. Faithful friends can help us face our issues and grow as a result. Their love and emotional support can reduce our sorrow, double our joy, and train us to become even better vessels of blessing for those we love. It can also strengthen our ongoing commitment as we seek to bestow the blessing.

ONE FINAL LOOK AT THE COST OF COMMITMENT

No doubt about it, commitment is costly. If you are serious about committing yourself to blessing those you love, expect to pay a price. Not necessarily in terms of money—a spouse and even small children are far too wise to be bought off with presents for very long. But you will need to invest time, energy, and effort to see the blessing become a reality in their lives.

Is the price worth it? The book of Proverbs certainly seems to show us that it is.

The final chapter of Proverbs describes a woman who blesses her family in many ways. She is industrious and loving, has a positive outlook on the future, and is committed to her husband and children. Her words to her family are filled with wisdom and kindness.

Did she just happen to be born this way? Certainly not. Each of these qualities was developed at a price. What is often skipped over when this passage is taught is how often this woman was up at dawn and how hard she worked to bless her family with her actions and words. She used the same kind of energy that gets parents out of bed on the weekend to take their children camping or enables a husband or wife to stay up late to help his or her spouse complete a project.

Was blessing her family really worth all that effort? It was for this woman. Read what her family has to say about her and her decision to make a genuine commitment to them: "Her children rise up and call her blessed; her husband also, and he praises her: 'Many daughters have done well, but you excel them all'" (Prov. 31:28–29).

It takes hard work, wrapped in the words *active commitment*, to provide the blessing to another person. It takes time to meaningfully touch and hug our children when they come home from school or before they go to bed. It takes courage to put into a spoken or written message those words of love for our spouses that have been on the tips of our tongues. It takes wisdom and boldness to "bow our knees" and highly value those we love. It takes creativity to picture a future for them filled with hope and with God's best for their lives. But all this effort is worthwhile.

One day, perhaps years later, the blessing that you give will return. Those you bless will rise up and bless you. What's more, you will find that the joy at seeing another person's life bloom and grow because of your commitment to seek their best is a blessing in itself.

Just ask one couple who took the time early on in their only son's life to provide him with the blessing. When he grew up, he would return words of blessing to them—in a most unusual way.

"Bubs" Roussel was only seventeen on that infamous Sunday morning in 1941 when Pearl Harbor was bombed. Later that day, he told his father and mother the shocking news of the Japanese attack.

Not long afterward, Bubs was called into the army and ended up serving in the Army Air Corps (now called the air force). After special training in communications, he was assigned as a radio operator in a B-29 bomber. The youngest in his crew, Bubs had to grow up fast. In only a few months he found himself stationed on the island of Saipan in the western Pacific.

From this tiny island, B-29s were making bomber runs on Japan. The work was dangerous, even deadly. On the morning of December 13, 1944, eighteen bombers soared out over the Pacific to make a bomb run on factories at Nagoya, Japan. Four of the planes that left Saipan that morning never returned. Bubs's plane was among them.

Official word that Bubs had been killed in action came to his parents from the War Department. They, like so many other family members in those days, received a telegram along with a small white flag, bordered with red and trimmed with blue and gold. The flag had one small gold star in the middle—the symbol of a son who has fallen in battle.

However, Bubs's parents also received something else. Almost a month after his plane went down, a letter came in the mail. Bubs had placed it on his pillow before his last mission.

Dear Folks:

I have left this with instructions to send it on to you if anything happens to me. I send you my love and blessings. My life has been a full one. I have been loved like very few persons ever. I love you all with the best that is in me. It hasn't been hard for me, knowing you believe in me, trust me, and stand behind me in fair or foul. Knowing this has made me strong.[3]

Would your children be able to write a letter like this to you? They could if they grew up in a home committed to being a source of blessings, homes like the one in which Bubs grew up. The words might be different, but the sentiment would be the same. Giving our children the blessing is like casting bread upon the waters. In years to come they, too, will rise up and bless us.

Gary's and my prayer for every person who reads this book is that you will become a person of the blessing. The cost is genuine commitment, but the rewards can last a lifetime and beyond.

For six chapters we have examined the various elements of the blessing and looked at homes that bestow that blessing on children. Unfortunately not all children receive a blessing they can give back to their parents. In the next section we will look at what happens in a home where the blessing is withheld, the painful consequences of such withholding for their children and later generations, and how those who have been denied the blessing can find hope and healing. This section might be especially helpful to you if you or someone you love is struggling with a lack of blessing in your lives.

However, if you are eager to get started *now* on making the blessing a part of your life, feel free to flip forward to part 4 of this book, which provides a wealth of practical guidance for starting down the blessing path and living out the blessing in your family's day-to-day activities.

 You have made it through part 2. Please go to TheBlessing.com/ Chapter 10 and watch a special video message from Dr. Trent as you start your journey.

PART 3

When the Blessing Doesn't Happen

ELEVEN

Homes That Withhold
the Blessing

WHEN I SPOKE about the blessing at a big Promise Keepers rally several years ago, I asked all the men who had missed the blessing to stand up so we could pray for them. We were in a huge football stadium, and it was packed. But when I made that request, literally half the stadium stood up. I suspect the same percentage would apply to most of our churches on Sunday morning.

So many men, women, and children are trying to get through life without the blessing their hearts yearn for. And if we are sitting next to someone like that in school or at work, if we are married to someone who missed the blessing, or if we missed it ourselves, it is important that we understand what we are up against.

The Mark of a Missed Blessing

Living for years with our families of origin leaves a profound mark on all of us. In most cases, this mark is a positive one, put there by a family that deeply cares for us and knows how to express that caring effectively. But some homes have serious problems that can deeply scar a man or woman. These homes can cause an individual to wear the mark of his or her family like the mark of shame God put on Cain.

Such people can spend years struggling to free themselves from their pasts and as a result are never free to enjoy a committed relationship in the present. If hurtful patterns from the past are not faced and broken, they are likely to repeat themselves in the next generation. Unfortunately this is where the terrible truth described in Exodus 20:5 becomes reality, and "the iniquity of the fathers" is passed down to the third and fourth generations.

In a later chapter we will look at how these hurtful patterns from the past can be broken. But first, in this chapter and the next, I want to introduce you to the six most common types of homes I see in counseling that withhold the blessing. In counseling couples and individuals all over the country, I have seen these six patterns surface time and time again.

Let me clarify before we begin our tour of these homes and common characteristics. In no way do I want this chapter to become ammunition to dishonor a parent or to blame all present problems on the past. Just the opposite is true. I hope that speaking truthfully and honestly about these homes and patterns will lead you to honor your parents (perhaps for the first time) and take responsibility for how you behave today.

Only when we can honestly look at our parents and our past are we ever truly free to "leave" them in a healthy way and "cleave" to others in present relationships (Gen. 2:24). If we are carrying around anger or resentment from the past, we are chained to the past and are likely to repeat it.

In gaining a better understanding of these homes that withhold the blessing and the characteristics they produce, we may also find we understand our parents' backgrounds better. Our parents were greatly influenced by growing up with *their* parents, and that experience affects us too. By looking at the types of homes our parents grew up in, we can often find answers to difficult questions about our parents that may have plagued us for years.

Most parents, I have found, truly love their children even if they do not know how to show it. Most have tried their best with the information and resources they had. Even in cases where that is not true—and there are such parents—it is possible to value them and forgive them just as God, in Christ, has forgiven us.

God's Word gives help and hope to deal with the lack of the family blessing, hope that doesn't come from dishonoring our parents or burying our heads in the sand and ignoring the past. Yet before we can look at a remedy, we need to understand the problems that exist. Only then can we be free to move forward in the present and to receive help so as not to repeat a painful past.

With this important caution in mind, let's look at the first kind of home that commonly withholds the blessing.

HOME #1: WHERE THERE IS EITHER A FLOOD OR A DROUGHT

In the springtime, the Seattle area is particularly beautiful—lush and green. Almost every day, clouds roll in and drench the land with refreshing rain showers. However, if you leave the city and travel only a few hours east, up and over the mountains that are set in from the coastline, you will observe a far different scene. These mountains do such an effective job in halting the rains that very few clouds get past them. As a result, the land on the east side of the mountains is actually semiarid.

We see a similar phenomenon in many homes today. One child, for what can be a number of reasons, will be drenched with lush showers of blessing from his or her parents. As a result, this child appears to thrive and grow.

Unfortunately, sitting just "east" of him or her at the dinner table can be one or more siblings whose emotional lives are like the parched ground. So few drops of blessing have fallen on the soil of their lives that emotional cracks begin to form. This very thing happened in one Old Testament patriarch's home.

We are already familiar with the patriarch Jacob and the fact that at the end of his life he gave each son a special blessing. However, the Scriptures paint real life, not Hollywood fiction, and the facts are that, when his children were young, Jacob showered only one son with the blessing: "Now Israel loved Joseph more than all his children, because he was the son of his old age. Also he made him a tunic of many colors. But when his brothers saw that their father loved him more than all his brothers, they hated him and could not speak peaceably to him" (Gen. 37:3–4).

That beautiful tunic may have spelled special acceptance to one son, but it brought out hatred from eleven brothers who were living apart from the blessing. Their anger reached such proportions that Joseph's brothers came close to putting him to death (vv. 18–22).

Anger, resentment, and insecurity are emotions that children who grow up without the blessing often carry—particularly when that blessing is so close, yet so far away. Like a thirsty man looking at distant rain, such children may experience discouragement and depression—emotional cracks and pain that quickly fill with persistent bitterness.

But it is not just the less-favored children who suffer in a flood-or-drought home. The one being showered with blessing can experience significant problems as well. We have seen this regularly in our counseling—where the one child who gained the blessing in a family feels guilty and defensive about receiving it.

Pro athletes and other famous people often have this feeling. Because of their outstanding abilities, they have been singled out for special praise far beyond what their siblings received. We talked to one athlete who felt this extra attention was a curse, not a blessing. He desperately wanted a close relationship with his brothers, but his parents' excessive attention to him kept his brothers at arm's length and left him aching with loneliness and feeling rejected inside.

Please don't misunderstand. Each child needs to be singled out sometimes for special praise or recognition. But if the elements of the blessing fall exclusively on one child, serious problems can develop for each child in the family. Just ask Joyce.

Joyce's parents were well-to-do educators at an outstanding university. After growing their careers for years, they finally decided they had room in their lives for a child—*one* child. But when Joyce's mother became pregnant, they were shocked to learn she was carrying twins.

Double the joy? Not for this couple. In their well-ordered, well-coordinated lives, there wasn't room for four. They would express their disappointment and anger in subtle and obvious ways throughout the girls' growing-up years. One twin, Joyce, was praised and appreciated while the younger twin, Janice, was scorned—a situation that brought resounding heartache to *both* children.

When children don't receive positive attention, they will look for it any way they can. And so Janice began, even in early grade school, to live up to her *unwanted* label. She did poorly in school, received worse marks in conduct, and brought home the kinds of notes and comments from her teachers that made her educator parents livid.

Finally, at age seventeen, Janice ran away from home with her latest boyfriend. "Good riddance!" was her parents' only publicly printable comment, and they quickly went back to blessing their oldest daughter. It would be more than twelve years before they heard from Janice again.

I met Joyce at a conference on the blessing at a large, metropolitan church. She came up to me during a break and told me the rest of the story.

Joyce had gone on to college, and her parents had even paid for her to complete a master's degree in music. She had then married and borne two beautiful children who sported their mother's and grandparents' red hair. But a terrible sorrow lay behind the joy in Joyce's life—all because of her sister.

For Joyce, the pain of being the one who received the blessing had been magnified a hundred times when her parents received a call from an AIDS clinic in New York. Janice had just died there—a prostitute who had contracted the deadly disease. The clinic had traced her back to her hometown through old letters and confirmed her identity through dental records. Janice had been so alienated from her family that, even in her dying days, she would not pick up the phone and call home.

Her parents refused to talk about what happened, but Joyce could not forget it. The joy of watching her children grow, the satisfaction of the education she received but her twin never got, the husband who loved her, the church she enjoyed so much—suddenly all those positive things seemed to be products of a terrible home, not gifts from a loving God. And all because she had been born seven-and-a-half minutes before Janice.

While this story is the most dramatic example I know of out-of-balance favoritism, I have heard literally hundreds of painful tales from people who have suffered in homes that play unfair favorites. Yet as we will see, there is hope for those from homes where the blessing falls on only one side of the mountain.

HOME #2: WHERE THE BLESSING IS HELD JUST OUT OF REACH

Robin's parents were both extremely demanding. Her father was a successful businessman, and her mother was a leader in social circles. "Success" was a motto in their home and had something to do with the title of every magazine they subscribed to. They demanded excellence from Robin and would only award praise or hugs upon spectacular achievement. What these parents didn't realize was that by placing the blessing up on the top shelf, their daughter grew up in a terrible double bind.

To please her father Robin majored in marketing in college, just as he had. She did quite well in school and landed a prestigious job with the chance for advancement. Robin spent many extra hours at her job, and her father was quite pleased with her achievements.

Then Robin fell in love and married a junior partner in the company. They had two little boys, who quickly became the apples of their grandmother's eye. But Robin's mother, who had never worked outside the home, expected her daughter to do all the things with the children that she had done.

Now Robin was pulled in two directions. To try to capture her father's blessing, she tried to keep the same pace at work that had won his praise in the past. To try to reach her mother's blessing, she tried to be Supermom and do everything with her children that a nonworking mother could do. After several years of a killing schedule, the pressure became too much, and Robin fell apart emotionally.

Our American culture is so fast paced that it is easy to be driven to the breaking point. Unfortunately, those who have missed out on the blessing are often susceptible to this kind of frenzied activity. In a misguided, often futile, attempt to reach for parental acceptance, they become workaholics. And make no mistake—workaholics are not just businesspeople. As Robin's story shows, there are also workaholic homemakers, mothers, volunteers—all struggling to gain attention and accolades that were always just out of their reach at home.

Christian leaders are not exempt either. Forgetting about God's sovereignty and biblical passages concerning our need for Sabbath rest[1], many modern-day pastors will work themselves until they drop. This is exactly what happened to a friend of ours in the ministry who never received the blessing from his parents.

Rick was what many considered a model pastor. Beginning his pastoral ministry at a small church that had not grown at all in fifteen years, Rick tripled the attendance and moved on to another church. Great success followed this move up the church-growth ladder, and he was pushed even further into the Christian limelight. After four years at his second church, working day and night to minister to the congregation, he was offered the senior pastorate at a megachurch with a membership of several thousand people. For a pastor in his denomination, he was on top of the mountain of success looking down.

Everywhere Pastor Rick went, more and more people would tell him how great he was. Then at age forty-six, an interesting thing happened to him.

Rick had raced home from the church one evening and wolfed down his dinner so he could go back to the church to lead a visitation team. He had hardly spoken to his wife, young son, or teenage daughter except for saying, as he stood up, "I've gotta run. It's visitation night."

As he turned to leave, his teenage daughter spoke up. "Dad . . . can I ask you a question?"

Turning toward her, he said, "Sure, honey, what is it?"

"Can you visit *our* family next week?"

Imagine climbing the ministry ladder to its greatest heights and waking up to the fact that your kids felt like orphans in their own home. But such is the cost to the children of confirmed workaholics who feel that if they ever slack off—ever—they will miss that blessing.

People who grow up with parents who always put the blessing just out of reach need to be introduced to a God who says, "My yoke is easy and My burden is light" (Matt. 11:30). In doing so, they can begin to serve people—and their families—with a whole new perspective. No longer driven to fill a gaping need for personal acceptance through other people, for the first time in years they can be freed for truly meaningful work and meaningful relationships. Even more, they can finally enjoy God's acceptance—not for trying to meet all the thousands of expectations around them, but just for breathing.

HOME #3: WHERE THE BLESSING IS EXCHANGED FOR A BURDEN

In some homes a form of the blessing is given to a child but at a terrible cost. Read the words of one woman who wrote a letter to a national columnist:

> Ever since I was a little girl, my mother made me feel guilty if I did not do exactly as she wanted. Dozens of times she has said, "You will be sorry when I am in my coffin." I was never a bad girl! I always did everything she requested me to do . . .
>
> Both my parents are eighty-two. One of these days my mother will die, and I am terrified of what it will do to me.[2]

This poor woman had paid a tremendous price for a blessing she is not even sure she has received. One certainly can't say she didn't try hard enough. Did you catch her words? "I was never a bad girl! I always did everything she requested me to do." In spite of all her efforts, she received a burden instead of a blessing.

In this third home that withholds the blessing a terrible transaction takes place. A child is coaxed by guilt or fear into giving up all rights to his or her goals and desires. In return, the child gets a counterfeit blessing that lasts only until the parent's next selfish desire beckons. So it was with Nicole, a woman who had to carry around a terrible secret in order to keep her blessing.

When Nicole was only nine years old, her parents divorced. Less than six months later, her mother remarried and a stepfather moved into the house. While Nicole's mother was away at work one evening, her stepfather came into her room. What started out as "play" became an evening of shame and horror for Nicole. Like thousands of young girls her age, she became the victim of sexual abuse.

The next morning, the stepfather pulled Nicole aside and told her that if she ever mentioned what had happened to anyone, he would beat her mother within an inch of her life, divorce her, and leave them both to "starve on the street." On the other hand, if she told no one, he would be nice to her and her mother and support them.

The fear of what would happen to her mother, added to her own feelings of shame, kept Nicole from telling what had happened. And her stepfather kept his part of the bargain. He went on with his life and marriage as though nothing had ever happened. He even treated her decently after that one event.

In remaining quiet to keep her stepfather's favor, Nicole thought she could buy her stepfather's blessing for her and her mother. But she paid a terrible price for her silence, living for years as an emotional hostage in her own home. Even after she grew up and moved away, her stepfather's cruel bargain still haunted her.

When I first met Nicole, she was married and the mother of three children. For years she had been living in another state and only saw her mother and stepfather infrequently, but she couldn't move past the hurt of her violation and enforced silence. Her painful memories shouted to her day and night to right this wrong. Only when she broke down and shared the secret with her loving husband did she begin to find freedom from this past burden. And only when she discovered her heavenly Father's love—given with no strings attached—did she begin to be healed of the damage that had been done in her life.

Parents who hold out the elements of the blessing to their child with such strings attached do them a cruel disservice. They are using one of the most powerful needs in the human heart—the yearning for the blessing—to lure a child into the web of their own selfish needs. The blessing we saw in the Old Testament was never purchased at such a terrible cost. It was a gift that was given, not something that had to be earned. If a blessing must be exchanged for a burden, it is not really a blessing after all.

HOME #4: WHERE THERE ARE EMOTIONAL MINEFIELDS

It was 1969, during the height of the Vietnam War, and my twin brother and I were sitting down with my father for lunch. This was a first! My father had left home when my twin and I were just three months old. We rarely spent time with him, and we had *never* gone to lunch with him. But Jeff and I were facing something that my father had gone through himself: the draft. So he wanted to talk to us.

"If your draft number is picked tomorrow," he said with deep concern, "you've got to know what you're going to face if you must go and fight." So over the next two hours, for the first and only time, I heard my father speak in detail about his experiences in World War II, as a young Marine on an island called Guadalcanal. Many of his stories from that day are still vivid in my mind, but in particular I remember his talking about the assignment he hated most—walking "on point."

Picture the scene. You are deep in the jungle, on patrol with a squad of soldiers. You are the "point man," the first one in line, and it is your job to scout for enemy soldiers and snipers and to watch for any booby traps they left behind.

You never know when a shot might ring out or your foot will come down on a camouflaged mine or if you'll trip over a wire that sets off an explosion that could cripple or kill you and your comrades.

Imagine the stress of each footfall—the tension never leaving you, the fear gripping your heart. And you have no choice but to keep walking forward, knowing the next step might be your last.

Many children grow up in a home that feels like that every day. It is a home full of emotional minefields and unseen booby traps that can blow up in a child's face at any moment. Things can seem perfectly fine at one moment and even go well for weeks or months, then something will set off an explosion. That's exactly what Steven experienced.

Like most teenaged boys, Steven would always head straight to the refrigerator when he got home from school. And most days, that would be fine. Steven could open the refrigerator door and eat or drink anything he wanted—even drink right from the milk carton—and his father, who was usually sitting at the kitchen table, wouldn't bat an eye. But some days his father would explode with anger if Steven even *reached* to open the refrigerator door. He would rant and rave about "eating me out of house and home" and slam the door shut, pushing Steven out of the way.

Steven never knew *when* such an explosion would occur. He could never be sure what would set it off. So he quickly learned the rules of living in a minefield. You never relax. You never invite friends over. And you never, ever walk into the house with an unguarded heart, because that may be the day that everything goes to pieces.

It's not only a father who can create such a home. In his inspiring and very honest autobiography, General H. Norman

Schwarzkopf tells what it was like growing up in a home with an alcoholic mother.

> I used to dread coming right home at night. I'd go around the side of the house, where there was a window that looked into the kitchen. I'd stand in the dark and look inside and try to judge what kind of night it was going to be. Mom had a Jekyll and Hyde personality. When she was sober, she was the sweetest, most sensitive, loving and intelligent person you ever met. But when she was drunk she was holy terror.

That terror was often vented on General Schwarzkopf's sisters.

> When Mom was drunk, a terrible meanness would come out, mostly in the form of personal attacks on my sisters. She might look at Sally and say, "Sit up straight! Why are you always slouching? Why don't you sit up straight at the table?" Then it would be "Just look at you. You're such a mess. Look at that hair." The small jabs would go on until she sensed she'd hit on something my sister was particularly sensitive about, and then she'd bore in until my sister broke down in tears.[3]

Such abuse is painful in itself, but the real damage in this kind of home comes from the unpredictability and the mixed message. One day a child will hear, "I love you. I care. I'm sorry." The next day those words are blown away with angry, explosive actions that say, "I hate you. You're ruining my life. You're the reason for my unhappiness." Growing up in such an unpredictable emotional environment can leave a child openly fearful of connecting with others or inwardly afraid of genuine commitment.

In 1 John 4:18, we read that "perfect love casts out fear." Yet for children who grow up in an emotional minefield, fear can reverse the equation and make them *less* loving. Often these are ACA (Adult Children of Alcoholics) homes, and they commonly leave scars that are felt for a lifetime. However, these homes are in neck-to-neck competition with a fifth kind of home that robs a child of the blessing.

HOME #5: WHERE UNFAIR FAMILY TRADITIONS RULE

Jim was confused and brokenhearted. At nineteen he had been ordered out of his parents' home by his father, and he did not know where to turn.

What was the problem? Was it open rebellion? Lying? Stealing?

Actually, for Jim's father, it was something even worse. Jim had a role he was expected to fulfill in his family, and Jim had decided not to fill it. Such an attitude is an unpardonable sin in homes that fly the banner "Unyielding Traditions Live Here." In this home the blessing is only given when a child chooses to go along with what is expected of him or her.

In Jim's case, the expectation was that he would be a minister. His father was a minister. His grandfather and even his great-grandfather had been ministers. Three generations of Smiths had heard the call to the ministry early in life and unquestioningly responded to it.

Now it was the fourth generation's turn. In fact, Jim's older brother was currently attending the seminary his father had attended. Jim, who had trusted Christ early in life and grown in his love for the Lord over the years, was now attending a Christian college in his hometown and dating a minister's daughter. Everyone assumed the next step for him would be seminary, then a small pastorate to continue his family's tradition.

Then Jim broke the news. He had finally declared a major in college, and it was marketing, not missions.

Jim's father was mortified. Having three generations of Smiths in the ministry and both sons in seminary or preseminary training had been such a good illustration in sermons and at conferences. Now he was in jeopardy of losing his bragging rights. All because his son had dared to question the unquestionable and break the Smiths' family tradition.

At first Jim's girlfriend was suspected of luring him away from his calling, but that proved to be false. His closest friends were all believers, and little evidence could be amassed that a conspiracy had been launched from that direction. No, it came down to Jim himself. In an angry session after dinner one night, he and his father exchanged words. Jim would not admit that sin in his life had led him astray, so his father "invoked discipline" on him. Jim was ordered to separate himself from his family until he had seen the error of his ways and repented.

Sound incredible? Such a separation is all too common when a child breaks a family's unwritten rules and bucks tradition. We have seen it with a son who refused to take over his father's garage, a daughter who didn't marry into the right social class, a son who dared to vote Republican, a daughter who turned down a bid to join her mother's sorority.

In each of these examples the parents felt cheated out of something they expected from their children. As punishment, they withheld or took back their blessing from that child. And this, again, can cause problems for every child in the family, not just the one who rebels. It can force a brother to choose sides, sisters to keep secrets. It can ruin every holiday and special family event because of the layer of ice that forms the moment the erring son or daughter walks in the door.

We need to be clear about what kind of parents we are looking at here. We are *not* talking about the kinds of parents who grieve over a son or daughter who has strayed into genuine error and they are forced to keep the child at arm's length for that reason. Eddie and Belle's oldest son, for instance, was an alcoholic. Don had started drinking in Vietnam, turning to the bottle to try to deaden the horrors of war. When he returned home, he continued to drink. He married and became a father, but he was unable to keep a decent job. When he began to take out his frustrations on his wife and children, she had to take out a restraining order against him.

Don's destructive behavior broke his parents' hearts, but they never withheld their blessing. They prayed for him daily and tried to be both counselors and encouragers. They helped him financially innumerable times and even bailed him out of jail on two occasions. But when he began physically abusing his family, they made the painful decision to withhold financial support unless Don attended an alcohol treatment program.

Eddie and Belle shared their decision with their son with love, but he exploded in anger. Calling them every name under the sun, he threatened to get even and stormed out of the house.

Don's parents did not stop loving their son. Yet because they loved him and wanted the best for him even more than they loved their relationship with him, they were willing to confront him and risk losing him for a season. They with-held one aspect of the blessing from their son because of the destructive problems he faced. Both biblically and relation-ally, they were on firm ground in doing this.

Such parents do not qualify to have the banner "Unyielding Traditions Live Here" raised over their home. Neither do parents who agonize over a believing son who is set on marrying an unbelieving woman or the parents who face the possibility that their never-married daughter may marry a man fresh from his fifth divorce. The kind of house that deserves this banner is reserved for people like Jerry and Elaine, who withheld every bit of their blessing from their daughter for reasons as solid as quicksand.

Brenda was a charming, intelligent young woman who deeply loved her parents. They cared for her, too, and had the material resources to express that affection in tangible ways—new clothes, new cars, the finest schools. These were hers until she met and fell in love with Brent.

Brent was attending the same distinguished school that Brenda was, but Brent was working his way through. Brent's father had died years earlier in a car accident, and his mother had raised him by working in a local grade-school cafeteria. Money was always tight for him, but he was doing extremely well academically and had a bright future ahead.

Brent and Brenda met the first day of school at the soror-ity house where Brent was *hashing* (cooking and cleaning up) to pay for his meals. Both Brenda and Brent were new believers in Christ, and they found they had many interests in common. Their relationship began as a close friendship, but by the end of the semester it had developed into something more. After a summer of e-mails and phone calls, they knew they had been smitten with the real thing. By December of the next year, they were talking engagement, and it was time for Brent to meet Brenda's parents.

Brent's mother lived near the college, and Brenda had met her numerous times. Already a deep affection was growing between the two. And Brenda just knew her parents would welcome Brent with open arms.

Nothing could have been further from the truth.

Brenda was so in love with Brent that she had failed to see the hardening attitude of her parents regarding their relationship. Not wanting to push her deeper into the relationship by forbidding it, they had hoped to coax her away from Brent by hosting parties and taking her to the club where all the *nice* boys were. But when Brenda phoned to tell them Brent was coming to visit, they laid down the law.

The little they had heard about Brent's background had been more than enough. Brenda's parents had too much at stake when it came to their daughter's social standing—and their own. He would never, under any circumstances, enter their home, much less become their son-in-law. In fact, she was to stop seeing him or lose their financial backing.

Though Brenda was devastated by her parents' attitude, she and Brent tried to pick up the pieces of shattered dreams. They sought counsel from their pastor and close friends and called on Brenda's family's pastor to ask his advice. Brenda even made a trip home to see if she could change her parents' attitude. They only repeated the firm warning that too much was at stake for her to throw it all away on someone who didn't "deserve" her or her family. As if being poor was not bad enough, Brent was a Yankee. Brenda's very Southern parents could not imagine that God's blessing—much less their own—would ever rest on such a person.

To try to honor Brenda's parents, Brent and Brenda put

off their engagement and marriage for a year and a half. During that time every attempt for Brent to meet her parents face-to-face or to discuss the issue was rebuffed. Finally, with a semester of school left, Brenda made the most difficult decision in her life. She and Brent were married at a lovely service in the small university chapel, with only Brent's mother in attendance. Brenda took a part-time job at the school bookstore to help pay for her final semester and graduation.

In the first seven years of Brent and Brenda's marriage, her parents visited her only twice, each time only to see a new grandchild. Their bitter rejection has never let up, nor have they ever given their blessing to their grandchildren. By withholding their blessing on Brenda's marriage, they have won a hollow victory. They lost the battle over whom their daughter would marry. But in their minds they win the war every lonely day and unhappy holiday that Brenda faces without their love and support.

It could be debated that Brent and Brenda should never have married in the first place, especially without her parents' blessing. But their ongoing bitterness, resentment, and unwillingness to make contact with their daughter's family— even years after the wedding—shows a desire to punish, not to stand on principle.

Homes like Brenda's that wave the banner "Unyielding Traditions Live Here" do not consider right and wrong—only rules and tradition. Parents like this know full well the impact of their punitive decision to withhold their blessing, and that is exactly why they do it. Their pride has been hurt; now their children will hurt as well.

In such homes the blessing is always conditional. Fulfill every expectation, and it will be given. Travel a different road, and a son or daughter can expect to wander far from the shelter of acceptance. This is the fifth home that commonly withholds the blessing, and it can leave a child emotionally in a place where it is always winter, never spring.

TWELVE

Half-Blessed

IN THE PREVIOUS chapter, we looked at five different home situations that can leave children bereft of the blessing. But there are other homes where a child does receive the blessing but only in part—usually because a parent is missing in action. There are several situations where this can happen, and each has the power to leave a child feeling only half-blessed. In this chapter we look at the most common of these situations and explore the impact they can have not only on the children but also on others in the family.

WHEN PARENTS DIVORCE

In the typical divorce the wife will retain custody of the children, and the father will move out. There are exceptions to this, of course, but it is still by far the most common scenario. And when it comes to interaction between the noncustodial parent (usually the father), certain changes are typical.

During the first year following a divorce, for instance,

many fathers see their children on a regular schedule. In fact, the "sugar daddy syndrome" is quite common, where the father smothers the children with gifts and attention right after the divorce. As a result, the children may feel closer to him than they have in years. (The one who usually has difficulty during this time is the mother, who may be struggling to make ends meet and has to compete with lavish gifts and trips for the children that she cannot afford.)

Unfortunately such attention is usually temporary. Typically, after about a year, the contact between father and child will begin to decrease. If he remarries or has to move away for business reasons, the change may be more dramatic. By the time three years have gone by, many fathers will see their sons or daughters once a month or even less often. They will be less involved in their lives, less aware of what they are thinking and feeling. And most likely, their ability and inclination to give the blessing will decrease.

Even if the custodial parent is diligent about giving the blessing—and a stressed single parent may find that a challenge—children of divorce are likely to grow up feeling partially blessed. They have the consistency of one parent's blessing and also the constant longing for the other's missing blessing. Anger, insecurity, and misbehavior can often result.

Again, not *all* fathers lose contact with their children after a divorce. And there are situations when the mother is the noncustodial parent. But the most important point is that children need the blessing from *both* parents. When one blessing is absent due to divorce, there will be a vacuum in a child's life.

We want to stress one important point to the parent remaining at home who consistently gives his or her child the blessing. (This point is also important to consider for parents of children who were deserted or adopted.) Children will naturally long for the blessing of the absent parent, regardless of the situation surrounding the divorce. Their desire for that missing element does not negate or devalue the blessing of the custodial parent. Almost all children have an emotional need to reestablish connection with the other person responsible for their birth.

I found this to be true in my life. My mother and father divorced when I was two months old. My mother retained custody of my older brother, my twin brother, and me, which gave her three children under three years of age to raise.

As I have had the opportunity later in life to look through books on how to be a good single parent, I have discovered that my mother could have been on the cover. To this day I cannot remember her running down my father verbally or erecting walls that would keep us from contacting him.

My mother worked full-time as an executive at a major savings and loan corporation, yet her nights and weekends reflected her commitment to us children. On dozens of Friday nights she would stuff us all in the car, hook on our little teardrop trailer, and off we would go to the mountains in northern Arizona or to the beach in Mexico to camp out with other families.

And you have to understand, camping was an acquired interest for my mother. She grew up in an affluent home in Indiana, and her only previous camping experience had involved Holiday Inns next to a campsite. Yet she knew that three growing boys needed the rigors of outdoor life and the male companionship of several married friends who treated each child in the camping club as their own.

I can say without question that my brothers and I learned about the blessing long before we could read about it in the Scriptures. All the elements of the blessing—meaningful touch, words of praise and affirmation, attaching high value, picturing a special future for each of us, and especially an unflagging commitment—were part of our experience with our mother. But my mother, a very loving person, was also very wise—wise enough not to be threatened when, after several years, my father sought to reestablish contact with us. She never used her blessing as a bargaining chip to play one parent against the other. I believe that is an important reason why, even in a home situation that is less than God's ideal, my brothers and I managed to grow up feeling loved and appreciated—though we still felt acutely the lack of our father's blessing.

I believe that any parents who are considering divorce need to face facts squarely. Splitting apart a marriage can affect each child in a severe and negative way. A growing marriage is the ideal place for children to receive a full blessing from their parents. But even when divorce cannot be avoided, both parents can make a big difference by doing their best to ensure that their children are not left half-blessed.

For noncustodial parents, that may mean working harder to stay involved in your children's lives, even when it is expensive or inconvenient, and being intentional (and creative) about providing the elements of the blessing when you are together. For custodial parents, that means recognizing that your children need both parents and doing whatever possible to facilitate an ongoing relationship with the noncustodial parent.

 Need a lift as you work through your personal blessing issues? TheBlessing.com has a wonderful section featuring new voices in Christian music—just click on "Music That Blesses Others." I'd especially like you to meet Shon Stewart, our host for "Music That Blesses Others." You'll be tremendously encouraged as you listen to Shon's music and his inspirational life story—as well as the music of others who choose to bless you with the gift of song.

DEATH AND DESERTION

In most divorces, both parents are still a factor in a child's life, even if one is missing on a day-to-day basis. But sometimes a parent or even both parents will be completely missing in a child's life because of death or desertion. This absence is something a child feels keenly, even if others do their best to make up for the lost blessing.

Desertion by a parent can be harder on a child than losing him or her to death. When a parent dies, a child knows that in this life the opportunity to obtain the blessing from that parent is gone. There is a certain closure although, of course, this depends on the age of the child. Also, while it is common for a child to feel anger at a deceased parent for leaving, the child usually has the consolation of knowing the parent did not do it purposefully. (A death by suicide may be a different matter and more closely resemble a desertion.)

The problem with desertion is that when a parent walks out on his or her children, they still know that "out there somewhere" is a living person who still has the power to bless. Some children even think they catch a glimpse of that missing person's face in an airport or on a crowded street. But when they run to get a closer look, the likeness disappears, and they are left face-to-face with a stranger. And they are left with the haunting knowledge that the missing parent *chose* to leave.

Desertion leaves so many important questions unanswered. It is a cruel dealer who passes out only half the cards a child needs to gain the blessing. And not surprisingly, this knowledge can have serious effects on a child.

In a seminar we attended on the effects on displaced children, one of the speakers used this quotation to describe how the desertion of a father can affect a daughter (the effects on a son will be different but still powerful):

> The father who deserts his family suddenly and never sees them again can leave a daughter forever afraid to allow herself to be vulnerable to a man, sure that he too will leave. . . . His daughter's resulting anger may give her trouble with men all her life. She may totally avoid men, or keep seeking the father she never had.[1]

With the Lord's help, such a prediction does not have to become a reality. However, nagging questions can remain in the mind of any child whose parents just walk out—questions Laurie asked herself for years.

Laurie's mother was having an affair with her supervisor at work. When he was transferred across the country, she packed her bags one day when the rest of the family was gone and went with him. She did not leave a note for Laurie or even call to talk to her. She just sent a certified letter addressed to Laurie's father, delivering notice of a pending divorce.

Laurie and her father did very well together through the grade-school and high-school years. She even went to secretarial school and landed a nice job as an executive assistant. Yet lurking in the shadows every time Laurie became serious in a dating relationship was a nagging fear. Every time she would think about marriage or having a family, a little voice would whisper, *Don't do it. You'll be just like your mother and leave them too.* Only with the counsel of a helpful pastor and learning about how God could meet the missing part of her blessing was Laurie finally enabled to marry and set up a happy family.

For more help with giving the blessing in special family situations, be sure and visit TheBlessing.com. You will also find stories and encouragement for singles who are committed to living out the blessing in their most important relationships, as well as special information for single parents and grandparents who are standing in the gap to bless a child.

DEALING WITH THE QUESTIONS RAISED BY ADOPTION

We see yet another group of children in counseling who commonly struggle with gaining only part of the blessing. These are adopted children who wonder why their birth parents never stayed to bless them.

We know many parents of adopted children who do a tremendous job of giving them the blessing. These parents more than make up for any loss a child might feel by being separated from his or her biological parents, especially if the child was adopted quite young. Yet in even the best of homes, where a child is totally secure in his adoptive parents' love, the question can still arise: "Why did my biological parents leave me?"

Sometimes this questioning comes in the form of misbehaving to see if the adoptive parents will "leave me like my birth parents did." These children will test the limits of their adoptive parents' commitment in an attempt to reassure themselves that they really are loved. Other children will do Internet searches or pay organizations to find their birth parents, all in an attempt to regain that part of the blessing they feel they have missed out on.

Adoptive parents should expect some behavior of this sort, especially when the child gets old enough to ask such questions. How the child responds will depend on the circumstances of the adoption and on the child's needs and maturity level. However, by providing the five elements of the blessing, backed by God's unchanging love, adoptive parents can give their children the security and self-confidence to face these questions in a healthy way. They may still ask the questions, but they won't be as dependent on their biological parents' blessing to lay the foundation for their lives. God's love, demonstrated for them through the family blessing, can bring them the certainty they need about themselves and the assurance that they belong to a family that truly loves them.

THE BLESSING IN A BLENDED FAMILY

As we travel across the country, we are constantly asked how remarriage affects the blessing. Many, many blended families do a wonderful job of giving the blessing to "yours," "mine," and "ours." But children in these homes are likely to bear significant hurts from whatever preceded the remarriage—divorce, death, living in a single-parent home—and bringing "steps" into the home can certainly complicate matters. For younger children especially, three reactions to this new family can lead them to actually try to prevent the family from blending, thus blocking the giving or receiving of the blessing.

First, almost all children will generate tremendous *expectations* concerning the possibility of remarriage, either negative or positive. Some children will expect the stepparent to be an interloper and resist all efforts to connect. Others may see the stepparent as an idealized person—someone who won't argue, someone who will make up for hurts in the past. (This is especially likely if there have been fights or negative behavior on the part of the natural parents.) When the child learns that, like anyone else, the new parent isn't perfect, anger and resentment can follow, again blocking a stepparent's blessing.

Second, children in a blended family often *fear* that accepting a new person into their lives is a betrayal of their natural, noncustodial father or mother. Family loyalties that go unaddressed can act like invisible stumbling blocks, making it difficult for a child to receive a new parent's blessing.

And finally there can even be *panic* in the heart of a child who fears that this new person (or persons if there are stepsiblings) will crowd out his or her place in Mom or Dad's heart. This is especially likely if several years pass before a remarriage. A child who is accustomed to being first in the parent's life can feel terribly threatened by a new person who is now competing for Mom or Dad's time.

At the same time that children in blended families are facing these issues, the parents and the entire family are likely to be going through significant adjustments—adjusting to a new home, creating new rules and traditions, and simply getting to know each other, as well as trying to parent effectively. In the midst of all the changes, it is easy for parents and stepparents to lose track of the need to be intentional in giving the blessing to natural children and stepchildren alike.

In all of these cases it is important to realize that you will never be able to outlogic the emotions. Simply telling them that they have no reason to be fearful or that they should not panic or feel disappointed doesn't erase the feelings. Patience and understanding are needed to draw these deep-felt issues out of a child's heart.

Helping a child receive and accept the blessing in a blended-family situation requires a concerted effort from both parent and stepparent. It also takes time. As our friend Dr. Robert G. Barnes writes, "The blend is a process rather than an end result."[2] But when parents and stepparents commit themselves to taking their new family down the blessing path—with meaningful touch, a spoken message, attaching high value, picturing a special future, and, above all, an active commitment to one another—they actually increase their chances of uniting as a family.

THIRTEEN

If You Missed the Blessing

IT SHOULD BE clear by now that helping a child receive and accept the blessing is of tremendous importance. But perhaps you have come to realize that you grew up in a home that withheld the blessing, and this realization has left you feeling hopeless. If so, take heart. You have the wonderful opportunity to overcome the past by extending the blessing to your own children. But first let's take a brief look at how missing out on the blessing may have affected you.

LIFE WITHOUT THE BLESSING

We have already looked at several examples of the challenges faced by people who missed out on the blessing when they were children. Let's examine a little more closely the ways that being deprived of the blessing can show itself later in life. Without the blessing, children can become . . .

The Seekers

Seekers are people who are always searching for intimacy but are seldom able to tolerate it. These are the people who feel tremendous fulfillment in the thrill of courtship but may have difficulty sustaining a relationship of any kind, including marriage. Never sure of how acceptance feels, they are never satisfied with wearing it too long. They may even struggle with believing in God's unchanging love for them because of the lack of permanence in the blessing in their early lives.

The Shattered

These are the people whose lives are deeply troubled over the loss of their parents' love and acceptance. Fear, anxiety, depression, and emotional withdrawal can often be traced to missing out on the family blessing. This unhappy road can even lead a person to the terrifying cliffs of suicide, convinced he or she is destined to be a "cipher in the snow."

The Smotherers

Like two-thousand-pound sponges, these needy people react to missing their parents' blessing by sucking every bit of life and energy from a spouse, child, friend, or entire congregation. Their past has left them so empty emotionally that they eventually drain those around them of the desire to help or even listen. When this happens, unfortunately, the smotherers understand only that they are being rejected. Deeply hurt once again, they never realize that they have brought this pain upon themselves. They end up pushing away the very people they need so desperately.

The Angry

As long as people are angry with each other, they are emotionally chained together. Many adults, for instance, remain tightly linked to their parents because they are still furious over missing the blessing. They have never forgiven or forgotten. As a result, the rattle and chafing of emotional chains distract them from intimacy in other relationships, and the weight of the iron links keep them from moving forward in life.

The Detached

Quite a few children who have missed out on the blessing use the old proverb "Once burned, twice shy" as a motto. Having lost the blessing from an important person in their lives once, they spend a lifetime protecting themselves from it ever happening again. Keeping a spouse, children, or a close friend at arm's length, they protect themselves, all right—at the price of inviting loneliness to take up residence in their lives.

The Driven

In this category, line up extreme perfectionists, workaholics, notoriously picky house cleaners, and generally demanding people who go after getting their blessing the old-fashioned way: they try to *earn it*. The thwarted need for affirmation and acceptance keeps these driven people tilting at a windmill named "accomplishment" in an illusory attempt to gain love and acceptance.

The Deluded

Like their driven counterparts, these people throw their time, energy, and material resources into the pursuit of anything they hope will fill that sense of emptiness inside. But instead of focusing on achievement, they look for social status, popularity, attention, and plenty of "toys." They never quite understand that the blessing is a gift that cannot be bought. Only counterfeit blessings are for sale—usually at an exorbitant price—and they last only as long as the showroom shine on a new car. So these folks are constantly feeling the need to trade in one fake blessing for another.

The Seduced

Many people who have missed out on their parents' blessing look to fill their relationship needs in all the wrong places. As we mentioned in an earlier chapter, unmet needs for love and acceptance can tempt a person to sexual immorality, trying to meet legitimate needs in an illegitimate way. Substance abuse and other compulsive behavior can also fall into this category. A drink, a pill, or a behavior is used to cover up the hurt from empty relationships in the past or present, and an addiction can easily result.[1] One study of compulsive gamblers (especially those struck with "lottery fever") found that over 90 percent of the male subjects had "dismal childhoods, characterized by loneliness and rejection."[2]

HOPE FOR HEALING

Do any of these descriptions sound even a little bit familiar? Perhaps you or someone you love has struggled to cope with the feelings or behaviors we have described—or someone else has pointed them out to you. (Sometimes it's hard to see in our own lives what is abundantly clear to others.)

If any of these scenarios ring true (or partially true), don't worry. There is hope and help for anyone to leave the ranks of those above and join the ranks of "the blessed." In fact, every missed element of the blessing can be regained. Rather than being locked into repeating the past, we all can find freedom to grow into the people God wants us to be.

In the rest of this chapter, we suggest some important steps that can begin the healing process. We are not offering a simple formula nor guaranteeing an instant cure. However, in counseling men and women all across the country, we find that many who have started with these principles have received hope and healing.

In our experience the road to blessing begins with the very difficult first step of being honest with ourselves.

HONESTY:
THE FIRST STEP TOWARD HEALING

Several years ago I counseled with the parents of a very disturbed twenty-one-year-old named Dean. He was angry and belligerent, occasionally violent, and his mental problems placed a tremendous burden on his family. And it was immediately apparent to me that they should have sought help long before they did.

These problems had first begun to appear after a car accident when Dean was eleven years old. The accident occurred soon after the family moved to Texas. Before the accident, when they lived in Michigan, Dean and his family had gotten along beautifully. In fact, they had been a model family at their church and in their community.

When Dean's behavior began to change following the accident, his concerned parents took him to specialist after specialist. They always received the same diagnosis: their son's problems had no medical solution. Perhaps time and understanding would work things out.

Instead, ten years after the accident, Dean was getting

progressively worse. But his mother, who loved him dearly, refused to recognize the severity of his problem. "It's just not that bad," she kept saying. "We just need to be patient."

Even when Dean was angry and sullen, she would spend hours trying to reason with him and read him verses of Scripture to make an impression on his life. Again and again she prayed that this "thorn in the flesh" would be removed and that their lives would be restored to what they were before the accident.

In an attempt to alleviate the mounting pressure because of Dean's behavior, she would often set up family socials and special holiday events. She wanted to re-create a time when the whole family could be "all together again, just like in Michigan." However, as soon as Dean arrived on the scene, he would ruin the party with his sulking and his outbursts.

Still, the mother held on to her denial. Her husband and the rest of the family could think what they wanted; she *knew* that things would get better. Life would once again be just like it was "in Michigan." She even dreamed about it—until one day her dreams turned into a nightmare.

Dean's father was nearing retirement, and the couple, who had saved up for years to buy a place in the mountains, was really looking forward to it. So six months before Dad officially retired, they called a Realtor about putting their house on the market.

Their children knew about the plan and were excited for them—except Dean. Though he had been living on his own for several years, he still made his parents' home his headquarters. This was almost a necessity because his violent temper had driven off every roommate and all but the staunchest of friends.

When Dean came to his parents' home one night and

saw the "For Sale" sign in their yard, he went berserk. He banged on the door repeatedly, but his parents were not home. Finally, he pulled up the sign from the front yard and used it to bash in the front-door window. Then he proceeded to tear up the house.

Dean's parents returned home several hours later to find the place in shambles—chairs overturned, lamps smashed, a potted tree ripped from its place and replaced by the "For Sale" sign. Upstairs and down, the house was a wreck.

Yet of all the damage Dean had done to the house, one thing in particular broke his mother's heart. Dean had gone to the hall where all the family pictures hung and cut every one of them to pieces. From baby pictures on up to their last family portrait with all the grandchildren, each one was torn beyond repair.

Dean's mother, like every parent, treasured her children's pictures. They were beyond price to her, especially the pictures of the family before Dean's accident. To her, those photos were a sign of hope that one day things would be just like before, just like "in Michigan."

Dean's mother finally had to recognize and acknowledge that just wasn't going to happen even if Dean made a dramatic recovery. She was forced to come to grips with the past and take responsibility for her present problems, instead of living with the dreams that Dean's problems would go away or trying to convince herself that the last ten years of Dean's outbursts really weren't that bad.

How does this story apply to those who have missed out on the blessing? Like Dean's mother, many will try to explain away and put off admitting the obvious in their lives. Drawing imaginary pictures of their pasts or denying the real problems that exist can often keep them from honestly facing their pasts and their parents. By protecting themselves or their parents, they effectively block their own healing.

Dean's mother refused to make the painful acknowledgment that her son had a serious problem, and she ended up suffering even more. People who put off coming to grips with their pasts often reap the same kind of harvest, a harvest where pain is multiplied and sorrows doubled, all because they refused to face the legitimate pain that comes with facing the truth.

SHINING A SPOTLIGHT ON THE PAST

John 8:32 is a Scripture verse that we require our counselees to memorize. It records the words of Jesus: "You shall know the truth, and the truth shall make you free." The truth about which Jesus speaks in this verse refers to knowing him in all his purity. Christ offers no cover-ups, no denying there is a problem when there really is one. When we know the truth, we walk in the light that exposes darkness and shows the way to freedom.

Many of us need to turn on truth's searchlight and shine it on our pasts. Only then can we be free to walk confidently into the future. Greg was able to do this, and it paid rich dividends in his life.

Greg was four years old when his parents told him a new little brother or sister was on the way. As with most four-year-olds, nine months seemed like nine years as he waited for his new playmate.

The day finally came when Greg's mother left for the hospital, and he knew he wouldn't have to wait much longer. That next day, Greg went with his father to the hospital to see his new baby sister. However, when Greg came into his mother's hospital room, he had a surprise. He had *two* baby sisters, two beautiful twin girls who were already the apples of their mother's eye.

Greg was certainly not loved any less when the twins came home, but life was certainly different. He now had to share his parents' time and attention with not only one sister but two. When the twins got older, things became even worse from Greg's perspective. The same people who stopped his mother to comment on how cute the little girls were in their double stroller rarely lifted their eyes to notice an older brother longing for the same affirmation.

Greg's parents loved him deeply. In no way did they intentionally try to overlook Greg or cater to the twins. And Greg loved his sisters. He was the perfect big brother, looking out for the twins and showing them the ropes when they got into school. Yet as the years went by, even the special bond between the twin girls became a minor source of jealousy for Greg. He just could not compete with the special closeness between his two look-alike sisters, and it bothered him.

Long after he and his sisters were grown and out of the house, Greg attended one of my seminars and heard for the first time about the family blessing. In many ways, Greg knew that he was loved and accepted and that his parents tried hard to provide him the blessing. Yet in his heart of hearts, he questioned whether he had really received it after the twins were born. For years he had a nagging insecurity in his life that he could trace directly back to this fact.

Greg knew that all his family would soon be gathering at his parents' house to celebrate the holidays. After the conference ended, he also knew that he needed to deal honestly with his feelings of missing out on at least a part of the blessing. With every bit of courage he had, Greg decided he would bring up the subject with his parents.

The first morning he was at his parents' home, the opportunity arose. The three of them were alone at the breakfast table; everyone else had gone out shopping for Christmas ornaments or a last-minute present.

Greg began talking with his parents by sharing with them much of what he had learned about the blessing at the seminar. The concept was new to them as well, and they perked up and got right into the discussion.

Greg then took several minutes to praise his parents and thank them for the way they had put several elements of the blessing into practice. Finally, in a loving, nonaccusatory fashion, he shared one of the deepest secrets of his heart— his feelings of missing out on part of the blessing after the twins came along.

As soon as Greg began sharing his concern, his mother began to cry. Greg immediately tried to comfort her and told her he wished he had never brought it up. "No," said his mother. "Please don't be sorry. I've wanted to talk about this for so long. I've always thought it might have bothered you, but I didn't know how to bring it up."

Almost instantly Greg and his parents were drawn into unity. They cried and laughed and hugged one another as if they had just come together after years of being apart. In a way, they had.

That night the now-grown children and their parents sat down for a family council, something they hadn't done in years. The topic of that morning's breakfast conversation was shared with the twins, and they had their chance to cry, to share, and to reaffirm their love for their brother and their parents. Any nagging guilt they had felt over the situation was now resolved and turned into gratitude for a courageous older brother.

Greg's willingness to share his feelings honestly with his parents and his twin sisters made a big difference—if ever a part of the blessing had been missing in his life before, it was certainly present now. Even his employer noticed the difference when Greg returned to work after the holidays a far more confident man.

We can't stress how important it is to be honest with your feelings regarding missing the blessing. It is the important first step to healing and restoration.

The Gift of Understanding

The next recommendation I would make to anyone who has missed out on his or her family's blessing is to understand as much as possible about his or her parents' backgrounds. Following this one bit of advice can free many people from wondering why they never received the blessing—something I discovered firsthand.

For years I felt pain about the relationship I had with my father. It would often be years between our visits, and he never made contact on his own initiative. His silence trapped a layer of hurt in my life that seemed untouchable . . . until I met Uncle Max.

He was my father's uncle—my great-uncle—but I didn't even know he existed until I went away to college in Texas. Max Trent, it turned out, was the head librarian at Southern Methodist University in Dallas. And as I got to know him, I took a big step toward really understanding my father—because Uncle Max told me so many stories I had never heard before.

I discovered what life was like at home when he was growing up. I learned much more about his war years and the personal and alcohol-related problems he had suffered as a result of those years. I learned that he had been deserted by his father, just as he had later deserted us.

Learning all these things was like turning on a light in a darkened room. I had often wondered why my father resisted communication with us. Now I saw numerous experiences that had shaped his behavior. I had never understood certain patterns he developed—and then I discovered they actually ran generations deep.

What I learned from Uncle Max was something I hope all children will take into consideration. In the vast majority of cases, parents who do not give the blessing to a son or a daughter have never received it themselves.

Andrea, like me, took this advice to heart, and it totally changed her perspective of her father. Andrea heard about the concept of the blessing at a singles' retreat where I spoke. For years she had struggled with how distant her father seemed. He was always cordial to her, and he never raised his voice with any of the children. But what was missing left Andrea with nagging questions about whether she had received the blessing. Besides an occasional hug, her father had not demonstrated, to her way of thinking, any of the five elements of the blessing she had learned about.

Andrea was still living at home, and she took the first opportunity she could after the retreat to talk to her father about what she had learned. What Andrea found out in that conversation turned out to be a key to understanding her father.

After her father had listened to his daughter talk about the blessing—he was always a good listener, just not a good talker—he cleared his throat and shared with Andrea something of his past. Andrea had never met her grandparents on her father's side. They had both died a few years before she was born. And as he had been an only child, Andrea had no aunts and uncles to pass down the family stories. So what her father told her now was news to her.

Andrea's father had grown up in England. His parents had even held claim to a small title of nobility. And they had their son raised with all the dignity and care afforded any English citizen of high birth. During his early years, he had a nanny who helped raise him, while his parents kept the respectable distance considered proper for teaching children discipline and manners.

His relationship with his parents was so formal that anytime he addressed his father, it was to be prefaced by Sir. There was no Dad, Daddy, Papa, or anything of the kind in this household. Sir was the proper form of address. Not surprisingly, meaningful touch was strictly taboo in that household, and words of praise were as rare as hen's teeth (which, in case you weren't raised on a farm, really are quite scarce).

In the course of one hour, Andrea learned more about her father's background than she had in the nineteen previous years. As a result of seeing how her father was raised, she gained a new compassion and understanding for his actions toward her and her brothers and sisters. She even found out that, compared to his parents, her father felt he was trying fanatically hard to make sure each of his children received the blessing. And all the time she thought he was withholding it.

If we will stop and take the time to look beyond our parents' actions during our childhoods to their pasts, it will be time well spent. We may even come to realize they need the blessing as badly as we do. And that realization can be the catalyst that frees us to seek the blessing from a more dependable source.

We shouldn't look down and lose hope if we grew up without the blessing. We should look up, instead, to the incredible provision of a blessing that can leave our lives overflowing, the kind of blessing that can even replace a curse with contentment.

[FOURTEEN]

Reversing the Curse

SOME CHILDREN HAVE difficulty relating to the entire concept of a family blessing because, from their perspective, they haven't just missed a blessing; they have actually received a curse. Something in their past has blocked the flow of good things into their life. Can such people ever move past this hurt and pain and genuinely feel loved and accepted?

If you had asked Helen this question four years ago, her answer would have been an emphatic no. In her mind, the pain she had endured from an abusive father had forever trapped her in a cycle of insecurity, fear, and unrest. Many times she had considered seeking a permanent solution to her pain, but she never quite mustered the courage to go through with it.

No one had to pay Helen's father to curse her. He seemed to enjoy making her life miserable. In fact, Helen would linger at the school library or stay at a friend's house as long as she could to avoid going home in the evenings. She would always hope her father had passed out from drinking too much. But all too often he was awake and propped up in front of the TV when she walked through the door. Then his "fun" would begin.

"Come over and give your father a hug," he would say when Helen tried to sneak past the living room door. She had no place to hide in her home. Her mother worked nights (and often stayed away during the day as well), and Helen was often left alone with her father. Without going into tragic details, Helen was repeatedly subjected to the physical abuse of a sick father. Always careful that he didn't leave visible marks, day by day he left heart-wrenching scars on his daughter's inner life.

Spending so many evenings in the library to avoid her father paid an unexpected dividend to Helen. She graduated near the top of her high-school class and gladly accepted a scholarship to an out-of-state college. However, physical distance does not equal emotional distance. Even though she was miles away in another state, Helen still spent way too much mental time in that living room next to her father.

Only after a number of years was Helen finally able to come to grips with her tragic past. She learned for the first time from a caring friend that God could take a curse from the past and turn it into a blessing. What Helen learned about God's family blessing is what we would like to share with you now.

THE POWER OF A CURSE

In biblical times, there was no mistaking the terrible power of a curse. It could freeze people in fear or drive them from a place of safety.

When David first met Goliath, the army of Israel was paralyzed by this giant's size and his evil words. Every day, Goliath would storm out and curse both the people of Israel and the Lord God. He kept the curses coming when young David went out to meet him. "Am I a dog, that thou comest to me with [sticks]?" he shouted at the youth. And then, for good measure, he "cursed David by his gods" (1 Sam. 17:43 KJV).

Years before that, when the Moabites realized that Israel had come up and camped against them, their king had summoned Balaam, a powerful warlock, and hired him to "curse . . . this people . . . that we may smite them, and . . . *drive them out of the land*" (Num. 22:6 KJV, italics added).

In Old Testament times, people took the power of a curse seriously. We should too. Because for people like Alan, the curse is real.

Alan grew up with a giant in his home. While his father's six-foot-three frame might not qualify him as Goliath, it certainly made him a giant to one small child who faced this man's terrifying anger. Alan would shudder in fear as his father towered over him and cursed him with angry explosions that inevitably left him in tears, often with toys shattered, and always feeling helpless.

Today Alan is taller than his father, but he still feels mouse-sized. The fear, anger, and hurt that were trapped in Alan's life caused him to struggle with truly feeling loved and accepted by God and all others in his life.

In Hebrew the word *curse* means to consider something of little value or worth. Like mist or steam, it is something of so little weight that, like a worthless irritation, it is to be brushed aside. In Old Testament times nothing was as powerful as a curse—except for one thing: a more powerful blessing.

Perhaps you, like Helen or Alan, feel cursed because of your childhood. In the next few pages we look at what a curse can do to you, how you can break its hold on your life, and who holds the only power to truly set you free.

CONSEQUENCES OF A CURSE

Living under a curse from a parent often leaves three tragic consequences that directly affect a person's future. A brief understanding of these three consequences and how to move beyond them is crucial if we are to ever learn to give and receive the blessing.

Consequence #1: Learned Hopelessness

The first common effect of living under a curse is illustrated in a research study done years ago at the University of Pennsylvania. Researchers made a surprising observation concerning animals. (Thankfully, such studies are forbidden by law today.)

For several months researchers conducted two independent studies with laboratory dogs. One group was put in a maze with various hurdles to climb over to reach their food. The average hungry dog would navigate quickly around the barriers and in under a minute would be chomping on dog biscuits.

At the same time another group of dogs were subjected to a pain tolerance test. These dogs were put in immovable, inescapable full-body harnesses and then subjected to strong electrical shocks—sixty-four random shocks in a sixty-minute period. Unable to move or to predict when the shocks would come, they were held prisoner in a painful situation.

With the pain study concluded researchers decided to use these same animals to run another maze test the next day. The scientists predicted that the dogs would quickly jump the barriers and get their food as the dogs before them did. Instead, when they ran into the first barrier, they simply lay down. Even when they were shocked to "motivate" them to jump over the barrier and move toward the food, they simply hunkered down, sat still, and endured the pain.

These dogs had not been critically, physically harmed by the shocks they had received. They had both the strength and the intelligence to get over the obstacles. But what had been shocked out of them was confidence, the willingness to even try. They had learned to be hopeless.

What were the conclusions drawn from these and a number of related studies? Namely, that uncontrollable, prolonged, negative experiences can freeze an animal, making him passive, pessimistic, and withdrawn in the face of obstacles.[1]

Drawing conclusions from animal research and applying them to the more complex reasoning of humans can be risky. But our experience in counseling, especially with those who have received a curse from their parents, shows some sobering comparisons.

There is no question that a major trauma, like losing a job or being mugged, can deeply affect us. And for some of us, the trauma of being cursed instead of blessed by our parents not only marks our pasts but immobilizes us as we face the future. It teaches us to be hopeless. Instead of actively trying to solve our problems, we can become passive, dependent, and depressed. And unfortunately, we can also live out two other negative responses to a curse.

Consequence #2: Chronic Pessimism

If we have labored under a curse from our parents, in addition to feeling a deep inner hopelessness when we face later trials, we can also begin to feel that there is absolutely nothing we *can* do to improve our situation. Pessimism becomes a habit.

Take Brian for example. He was the older son of a man who favored the younger. In Brian's thinking, if Dad had to make a choice, he should have bonded with *him*, not his little brother. He wore his heart out trying to please his father. But no matter how far he stretched toward the man, he could never reach the arms of acceptance he wanted.

In this climate of unfair comparison and favoritism, Brian made a subtle but terribly damaging decision. Deep inside, he equated his missed blessing with something he could never become—*younger*. And because he focused on something that could never happen as his key to future happiness, he became a committed pessimist in the present. He eventually pushed himself right into clinical depression!

The defining mark of a pessimist is to look backward.[2] For example, a pessimist looks back, wanting to be younger, while an optimist looks forward and wishes he or she were older! By never being able to forget what lies behind, pessimists stay stuck in their pain, rather than looking forward to a positive future.

Listen to a more humorous example of someone who illustrates this point. It is taken from an actual letter we received.

I'm thirty-four years old, and I've been married three times. (Not my fault; always seem to pick losers.) My problem is my hair . . . or lack of it.

I know that many men feel there's nothing wrong with being bald, but I do. I started losing my hair when I was in high school and have since tried everything I know to stop what's happening to me. I know that my first wife left me because of my hair. My latest wife even told me straight out that I was obsessed with my hair, and that was why she was leaving. *My lack of hair is ruining my life!* I went to a plastic surgeon recently and offered to pay him, in advance, to transplant whatever skin I needed to fix my hair. All he did was insult me by saying that I shouldn't waste my money on scalp surgery, but should spend the money on a psychiatrist!

I'm sure that doctor wasn't a Christian. That's why I'm writing you to ask your advice. . . .

When it comes to facing the future, this man has a major problem. In his mind (or actually on top of his mind) is something that forever keeps him from finishing first in life or even coming in a strong second. He simply can't picture a successful future for himself without thick, curly locks of hair. And by picking out something that he is powerless to change and making it the source of all his problems, he directly affects his future.

If we have labored under a curse that makes us feel powerless and if we believe the only key to change is forever out of our reach, there is a final consequence.

Consequence #3: Lonely Withdrawal

During the experiment we described earlier, the dogs who had been shocked were verbally, then physically, encouraged to jump the barrier when they ran the maze. But it didn't help. They drew so far into an inner, protective shell that the fear of more pain made them oblivious to outside encouragement.

We have seen this same type of behavior so often in people we've counseled.

Take just one example. Jim remembers a Sunday when he was nine years old and sitting next to one of his friends at the back of the church. His father was the preacher and, in the middle of his sermon, he saw the two boys whispering to each other. Suddenly the father's voice rang out through the church, ordering his son to come up front. Before the entire congregation, he laid into Jim about what a disrespectful and dishonoring son he was. Then he stopped the service, took Jim outside (but in full view of the congregation from the windows), and gave him a whipping he's never forgotten.

Many years later Jim still carried the effects of many episodes like this where he received a curse, not a blessing, from his father. As an extension of the pain and powerlessness he felt as a child, he would become almost comatose if his wife spoke in anger, asked for change, or said anything that could be remotely interpreted as criticism. When he saw her negative words coming, he would beat a hasty inner retreat. And instead of responding to her pleas for help, he just pulled further inside—which made her even *more* vocal and frustrated.

Needless to say, Jim's withdrawal contributed to a deep sense of loneliness and isolation for both husband and wife. By the time the two of them got into counseling, their marriage was crumbling.

If we believe our efforts do not count, if the key to change seems out of reach, and if we feel a deep sense of loneliness and isolation, chances are we are still laboring under a curse from the past. But there is a power stronger than any curse.

 If you missed out on the blessing during your childhood or even felt cursed by what happened to you as a child—or if someone you love struggles with these issues—be sure and visit TheBlessing.com for additional hope and help.

WHAT IT TAKES TO REVERSE A CURSE

There was a power that young David drew on that kept his heart from freezing in fear when cursed by Goliath. And when the mighty warlock Balaam was hired to curse God's people, someone acted to not only frustrate Balaam's words but to turn them completely around.

Who was it? The prophet Nehemiah gave the answer centuries later, at the dedication of the wall in rebuilt Jerusalem after Israel returned home from captivity. He told the great story of someone even more powerful than Balaam who could not only stop but also reverse the curse: *Almighty God*. We are told that God not only frustrated Balaam's effort but also "turned the curse into a blessing" (Deut. 23:5 KJV).

Turning wrongs around is something God specializes in, particularly for those who have received a curse in their homes as children. But how? Briefly, here are three necessary elements for lifting a curse from a life.

Curse Lifter #1: A Commitment

If some of us have learned to be hopeless through shouldering a curse in the past, then the first step toward reversing the curse and learning to be hopeful comes from making a wholehearted commitment.

Several years ago I worked with a man who had carried the curse of hurtful words for years. While it's driven him to succeed, it's never left him with a moment's inner rest or peace. As part of our conversations I asked him clearly if he had ever truly committed his life to Jesus Christ. "Absolutely," he said. And while he had only recently trusted Christ, he bore a strong, convicting testimony.

"Do you want to be the husband and father God would have you be? And are you willing to do whatever it takes to be the man God wants you to be?" Again, the answers were a resounding yes.

"Would you put that commitment in writing?" I asked. And he did.

Since that day, for more than a decade now, that single sheet of paper has hung in his office. For him it has been an important milestone in overcoming the curse he has been under.

One of my favorite verses in all of Scripture, and the first I memorized as a new Christian, is 2 Corinthians 5:17: "If anyone is in Christ, he is a new creation; old things have passed away; behold, all things have become new." A key to sorting out the inner confusion that comes with receiving a curse is making clear, definite commitments. Then once we have made those commitments, we begin to gain the following characteristics.

Curse Lifter #2: Self-Worth and Self-Control

One glaring problem that surfaces for those I counsel who have grown up with a curse is a lack of self-control. And not surprisingly *the degree of self-control in an individual is directly proportional to his or her self-worth.*

The lower the value we have of ourselves (remember, the word for *curse* literally means "of little value"), the less energy we will have to discipline our attitudes, appetites, and actions. We will reward ourselves with junk food, instead of consistently exercising; let five hours a night go by before we finally turn off the television and stumble into bed; or procrastinate on those things we must do at work.

Out of strong commitments comes renewed energy to view ourselves differently, more positively, and we gain more self-discipline and self-worth as a result. And that positive result is increased as we gain something else.

Curse Lifter #3: A Clear Challenge

For those of us who have labored under a curse, our God can break its impact on our lives, renew our commitments, and restore the energy to be self-disciplined. One way he does that is to give us a clear challenge.

Many studies have shown how crucial it is to maintain a clear purpose and challenge in life. In fact, many of these studies center on the fact that the only challenge most men have is their work. That's why the average man in the United States dies within three years of retirement! (A classic example was Coach Bear Bryant, the great University of Alabama coach who died *three weeks* after retiring from over fifty years of coaching football.)

The Scripture is true, "Where there is no vision, the people perish" (Prov. 29:18 KJV). Yet the future painted for many people who have grown up with a curse is anything but clear. What they need is a purpose, something to work toward, a reason to move forward.

How clear is your purpose in life? Do you have a challenge that is big enough to last a lifetime? To move you forward each day? You do if you are seeking to give the blessing to others. *For one of the most powerful ways of reversing a curse you've received is to give the blessing to others.*

For the Lord, the opposite of the curse was giving his children the blessing. As his servants we are called to be a blessing to all the earth. The elements of the blessing that we have detailed in this book provide you with a simple, biblical plan to bless your children, spouse, friends, and others.

Commitment, self-control, and a significant, therapeutic challenge to be a blessing—these are the three things that can help break the negative cycle of the curse. They are the very things God desires for your life.

Look at God's Word to see just what kind of future he calls you to. As he looks at you, he sees a future totally free from a curse: "For I know the thoughts that I think toward you, says the LORD, thoughts of peace and not of evil, to give you a future and a hope" (Jer. 29:11).

To give you this future he calls you to commitment. He confirms your self-worth and moves you toward self-control. And he challenges you to do something great in your life—to share the blessing. But he offers you the gift of his blessing as well—his spiritual family blessing that can reverse the curse and open the door to overflowing blessings in your life. All you have to do is trust in him, and he will do the rest.

An Open Door of Blessing

Some children, like Helen, will never hear words of love or acceptance from their parents. Others, like Alan, will try and fail to break down the door to their parents' hearts and receive the blessing. For whatever reason they have to face the fact that their blessings will have to come from another source.

When Helen finally realized this and turned to listen to the voice of her heavenly Father calling her, she discovered an open door of blessing. She found a spiritual family blessing that provided her with every element she had missed while growing up. This blessing was the key to reversing her curse—just as it is for any believer.

As Believers, Our Spiritual Parentage Is Secure

Helen was never secure in her relationship with her father. His anger and abuse had frozen within her heart a sense of mistrust and insecurity. Yet when Helen trusted Jesus Christ as her Lord and Savior, she found that she had a source of blessing that would be with her each day of her life and beyond! Helen discovered verses like these that speak of how stable and kind her heavenly Father is and how permanent her relationship is with him:

> My sheep hear My voice, and I know them, and they follow Me. And I give them eternal life, and they shall never perish; neither shall anyone snatch them out of My hand. (John 10:27–28)

> And Jesus came and spoke to them, saying, ". . . Lo, I am with you always, even to the end of the age." (Matt. 28:18, 20)

> For He Himself has said, "I WILL NEVER DESERT YOU, NOR WILL I EVER FORSAKE YOU," so that we confidently say, "THE LORD IS MY HELPER, I WILL NOT BE AFRAID. WHAT SHALL MAN DO TO ME?" (Heb. 13:5–6 NASB)

> The Spirit of the Lord GOD is upon me, because the LORD has anointed me to bring good news to the afflicted; He has sent me to bind up the brokenhearted, to proclaim liberty to captives, and freedom to prisoners; . . . to comfort all who mourn, . . . giving them a garland instead of ashes, the oil of gladness instead of mourning, the mantle of praise instead of a spirit of fainting. So they will be called oaks of righteousness, the planting of the LORD, that He may be glorified. (Isa. 61:1–3 NASB)

The first thing Helen had to consider when she came home at night was what kind of mood her father would be in. One night it would be anger, the next indifference, and occasionally he could even be very nice. His vacillations kept her off balance, leaving her insecure and questioning herself. Now she had a relationship with a heavenly Father characterized by the words "Jesus Christ is the same yesterday and today, yes and forever" (Heb. 13:8 NASB).

Those who have personally believed in Jesus and trusted their lives to him have a secure relationship with their heavenly Father. Yet there is even more to God's spiritual family blessing that they receive when they trust their lives to him.

As Believers We Gain a Spiritual Family to Bless Us

In chapter 6 we told the story about a little girl who was very scared and needed "someone with skin on" to hug her. As we saw in that chapter, our Lord knows all about our need for meaningful touch. He also knows our need for the physical companionship of others to build up our lives and encourage us.

That is why when we accept Christ, we gain not only a secure relationship with our heavenly Father, but we join an entire family of brothers and sisters in Christ! Men and women "with skin on" who can hug us and hold us and communicate God's love, wisdom, and blessing to us!

In many ways the early church provided a very good model for us to follow. They were often in each other's homes (the earliest churches started in homes) and shared meals together. They were literally a family of the faith, and that is just how Paul expected Timothy to treat the believers he met. Listen to the counsel this noted apostle gave his younger charge: "Do not rebuke an older man, but exhort him as a *father*, younger men as *brothers*, older women as *mothers*, younger women as *sisters*, with all purity" (1 Tim. 5:1–2, italics added).

Timothy was not related to these people by physical birth, but Paul pointed out clearly that he was related to them through spiritual birth. They all shared the same heavenly Father, and they were all necessary members of one another.

For both Gary and me, this principle of having spiritual family has been a tremendous personal help, particularly the way God used an older man in each of our lives to become a spiritual father to us in times of need.

Gary was in college when his father died, leaving a huge vacuum in his life. At this crossroads period in his life, a godly man named Rod Toews stepped in and became a spiritual father. Rod is a nationally prominent speaker and Christian educator. He could have easily let his busy schedule crowd out time for a hurting collegian. However, Rod attached high value to Gary and took him under his wing to shepherd and support him. Both verbally and by his presence at a critical time, Rod gave Gary the blessing that was missing after his natural father had died.

I was a freshman in high school when I met a man who would become my spiritual father. Doug Barram, at the time a Young Life area director, had come to watch a freshman football game. Besides a few parents who were dyed-in-the-wool fans, *nobody* goes to freshman football games. Yet Doug was there, standing along the sidelines at every game, offering words of encouragement to a young man who had not yet heard about Christ.

In the years that followed, this man took a fatherly interest in my two brothers and me, giving spiritual support to three boys from a single-parent home who very much needed it. Each brother and even my mother would eventually come to know Jesus Christ—and all because of Doug's deep love for his Savior, a love that was reflected in his fatherly love for us.

To return to Helen's story, she had a similar experience in learning how God's family can become a source of the missing blessing she sought. In her case, that blessing came with a spiritual sister she met at work.

Helen worked in the accounting department of a major oil company. When a woman at the office retired, Karen came to take her place. Karen was a committed Christian who had prayed God would provide the opportunity for her to share his love with someone in her new office. That someone turned out to be Helen.

Karen was a mystery to Helen at first. She always seemed to have such a positive attitude and calm spirit, even when there was great pressure at work. Perhaps more than anything, it was Karen's inner peace and lack of anxiety that made Helen want to be around her.

Soon Karen and Helen had struck up a friendship and were sharing stories about the rigors of dating and their frustrations at work. But Karen also began sharing with Helen the good news about a heavenly Father that Helen could come to know. At first Helen didn't want anything to do with such talk. She had had enough of fathers to last a lifetime. Yet gradually, in spite of herself, the Holy Spirit worked through Karen's life to draw Helen to a saving knowledge of Christ.

Karen took Helen to church with her for the first time in Helen's adult life. Helen couldn't believe what happened. She was asked to stand up as a visitor, and she was greeted by the pastor. After church a number of people stopped her to say they were glad she had come. One elderly lady even hugged her. Helen then went with Karen to the singles' Sunday school class. People shared prayer requests before a short message; then they actually held hands and prayed for one another.

Helen found people who had never laid eyes on her treating her like a sister and encouraging her to come back. For the first time in her life, she saw the source of blessing a church family could be, and God used that experience literally to change her life.

Any person who has missed out on all or part of their parents' blessing—even one whose experience as a child qualified as a curse—can acquire a spiritual family of fathers, mothers, brothers, and sisters to fill the void and help heal the wounds. With a secure personal relationship with a heavenly Father and a spiritual family that offers warmth, love, and acceptance, every element of the blessing can be ours.

As Believers We Are Called to Give the Blessing

Just in case you have forgotten (or are one of those readers who begin a book in the middle), let's review the five elements of the blessing:

1. Meaningful touch
2. A spoken (or written) message
3. Attaching high value
4. Picturing a special future
5. An active commitment

Karen provided each element of the blessing to Helen, and it brought Helen to the Savior and to his church. By introducing Helen to a loving group of friends at church, Karen was able to see her blessing multiplied as many people took an interest in Helen's life.

God has equipped the church, the local body of believers, to provide each aspect of the blessing to people in need. Where churches are growing, you will find a body of believers who are practicing these five elements of the blessing. These are also the churches that are drawing in the unsaved, not simply luring other believers away from the church down the street.

That was the kind of church Helen found herself part of—and three years of being part of that congregation brought tremendous changes for her. She had gone from feeling isolated and alone to feeling truly blessed for the first time in her life. Helen could finally rest in the shelter of her caring friends at church and forget about the past, right?

Not quite. Her life still needed to go full circle.

Helen had received God's blessing from others. Now she needed to become a source of blessing to others around her. And she did! For the first time in her life, she began to think of her coworkers and the people in the office and at her apartment building in terms of what she could give to them, not just what she needed from them. Because her life was filled with God's blessing through his Spirit and his people, she could love and serve them without expecting something in return.

Helen had eaten fully and drunk deeply from the feast of life God had provided her in his blessing. However, one final thing was left for Helen to do if she truly wanted to be free from her past. She needed to become a source of blessing not only to her friends and acquaintances at church and at work, but to her enemies as well—and one enemy in particular.

For Believers, Blessing Means Forgiving

As incredible as it may seem, Helen needed to become a source of blessing to her father—the very one who had caused her so much pain and had caused her to begin to search for acceptance in the first place.

"Couldn't I just skip over this part?" Helen asked her pastor when she learned about her need to bless her father. Yet in her heart of hearts she knew she would never be truly free of his grip over her life until she could do this.

It took her awhile to get there. She had to go from adamant refusal to quiet acquiescence to firm resolve to wanting to chicken out at the last minute and finally to getting on a plane to go see him.

It turned out to be the second most meaningful day in her life.

Her most meaningful day was when she met the Lord Jesus, the One who changed her life by meeting her missing need for him and giving her his love and acceptance and blessing. Coming to Christ also gave her a spiritual family to bless her in the present and provided her with the power to truly break free from the yoke of the past.

Jesus is the person who can change our lives and the lives of loved ones who are struggling without the blessing by providing us and them with God's spiritual family blessing—a blessing that is not just for parents and their children but can enrich marriages, intimate friendships, and relationships within the church family.

 You have made it through another section. For a video message from Dr. Trent about missed blessings and healing, be sure and visit TheBlessing.com/Chapter 14.

PART 4

Living the Blessing Challenge

FIFTEEN

First Steps: A Written Blessing

THE TWO THIN, watermarked sheets of white stationery are now folded down into a small square. I carry them in the safest zippered part of my backpack, which goes with me everywhere. The writing on the paper is starting to fade, and I keep promising myself that I'm going to make a copy of it. But I haven't done it yet—because the paper was his. The writing in black pen was his. The words I had longed to hear all my life were his.

Those two small sheets headed simply by a date: December 1986. They contain some of the most encouraging words I have ever received—a blessing beyond price to me. They came to me unexpectedly. But they are an example of something we are going to challenge you to think about, plan out, and pray over.

You have now spent a number of chapters understanding how important the blessing can be. You have gained a clear picture of each of its five elements and their impact on a person's life and future. Now it's time for ground school to end and flight school to begin. We believe you are ready to fly solo and soar now. In this chapter we ask you to take your first step of the blessing challenge by first writing out a formal blessing for your child and then sharing it with him or her.

WHY WRITE?

As we have seen in earlier chapters, both the spoken word and the written word are important in giving the blessing. For several reasons, however, we are suggesting that you put your words of blessing into written form *first*, before you share them out loud with your child.

First of all, ideally, your written blessing will *also* be spoken—we will include ideas for doing that below. But writing your words out first can take away a lot of pressure. You have the opportunity to put the words together at your leisure. You can double-check that you have included all the elements of the blessing and that your words convey exactly what you want. And if your words have been chosen ahead of time, when you do speak your blessing, you can concentrate on connecting with your child.

Another reason to write out your blessing, though, is that a written blessing can be saved. The words can be read and reread, and the paper it is written on can be tucked away as a keepsake. (Even e-mailed blessings can be stored and reread.) Written blessings can also be sent by letter or e-mail and thus cover great distances. A written blessing has the capacity to bring warmth and light and love to your child again and again throughout his or her life—far beyond the mere ink marks on paper.

That's what the letter I carry in my backpack does for me. But to understand that, you need to hear a little more of the story. It is about my Uncle Max, whom I mentioned in an earlier chapter.

I met Uncle Max when I moved from my home state of Arizona to attend Texas Christian University (home of the mighty "Frogs") in the city of Fort Worth. In one of my English composition classes, I was assigned a topic for a major paper by my professor. The only problem was after he assigned the topic, he told me our library at TCU didn't have what I needed to complete it.

"Do you have a car?" the professor asked. When I replied that I did, he explained that the best place for finding information on my topic was to drive to nearby Dallas and use the library at Southern Methodist University. Apparently, they had a "plethora" of articles and books on the subject.

Not sure exactly what a plethora looked like, I made the drive on a Saturday and parked next to a beautiful redbrick library. (The whole campus at SMU is beautiful.) I walked inside and was headed toward the reference desk when I saw it—a nameplate on a glass door, right next to the reference desk. The nameplate read, "Robert M. Trent, Head Librarian."

The door was almost all the way open, and a man was sitting inside—presumably the head librarian himself. Spontaneously, I thought of something funny to do. I stopped, stuck my head in the door, and said, "Hi, Uncle Bob. I'm your long-lost nephew, John Trent, from Arizona."

It was a totally throwaway line. Sure, we shared the same last name, but I had no reason to believe we were actually related. I was sure he would just look puzzled or slightly annoyed at being interrupted, and either response would have been fine with me. What I wasn't ready for was his next question:

"Are you Joe Trent's boy?"

I was dumbfounded. You see, at that point, I had essentially no relationship with my father. I had met him only once, and not under the most encouraging circumstances.

And I knew exactly *none* of my relatives on my father's side of the family. I did know my father was from Indiana, but the possibility that he had relatives in Texas had never crossed my mind. So walking right into the office of my great-uncle—*my father's uncle*—was a total shock.

I soon learned that he went by Max, not Robert, and he was extremely gracious to invite me into his office for a conversation. After we talked a good while, he picked up the phone and called his wife—my Aunt Sally, it turned out. To my surprise, while he was on the phone, he asked Aunt Sally if she had cooked enough to invite me home for dinner, and then he held the phone down and asked me if I would join them. So began a relationship that became one of the most important in all my life.

Uncle Max and Aunt Sally had no kids. They had books. Both held PhDs from Columbia University, and both were head librarians—she at the Dallas Public Library and he at SMU. Over the next twelve years, during my college, seminary, and graduate school days, they became my Texas family. They would invite me over for holidays if I couldn't go home to Arizona and have me over often for a weekend meal. Uncle Max spent hours talking to me about my father—opening up doors into his life that I had never been aware of and never would have discovered from any conversation I ever had with Dad.

It was Uncle Max, for instance, who told me that my father had been abandoned by *his* father—what a shock that he would grow up and do the same thing to my brothers and me. Uncle Max also told me about my father's war experience and its aftermath—the Bronze and Silver Stars he earned from fighting at Guadalcanal, the wounds that sent him home more dead then alive, the nightmares that drove him to drink. As I learned more about my father's life, I found it harder and harder to hate him. In fact, I owe it all to Uncle Max that I finally met with my father and asked forgiveness for being so angry with him for so long. Not so he would change—he didn't—but so that I could untie the knot and be free from hating him.

Uncle Max and Aunt Sally helped me a lot during those years, including modeling for me something I had never seen up close—a good marriage. Then came that terrible day when a double-wheeled wrecker hit Aunt Sally, sending her to the hospital in critical condition. Uncle Max and I arrived at almost the same time. On top of her traumatic injuries, she had also suffered a heart attack from all the pain and stress of the accident.

Uncle Max had given me so much in terms of warmth and love and information and understanding. Now I had a chance to give back what I could to him. For four days and nights I stayed with him at Baylor Hospital, praying the whole time. Praying for him. And praying for Aunt Sally, who was his whole life—and who, we had been told, wouldn't make it through the first night.

But she did make it through that first day and night. Then a second. Then a third. And then the doctor came into the waiting room where we were sleeping on the fourth morning. He told us that he had just finished his early morning rounds and that Aunt Sally was going to be all right. In fact, it was miraculous the way she had rallied.

Uncle Max and I hugged and cried, and I prayed and thanked the Lord for his grace in healing Aunt Sally. Then Uncle Max asked me to pray one more time. Actually, first, he asked me to explain to him more clearly just who I had been praying to those four days. And then he wanted me to pray again as he accepted Jesus into his heart so he could thank him for Aunt Sally's healing too.

Four years later Aunt Sally passed away in her sleep. By that time I had moved back to Arizona. But Uncle Max and I stayed close. We talked often, and I would see him whenever I was in Dallas.

Then one day, out of the blue, I got a letter—the same two-page note I still carry in my backpack. "Dear John," it began, "I know it is going to come as a surprise to learn that I have drawn up a living will. . . ."

He went on to detail his last wishes and give me instructions for retrieving his will from the lawyer. That's how I found out Uncle Max was dying of cancer. But then on the second page, in the last paragraph, come those incredible words of blessing—those unexpected words I have treasured and carried with me every day since.

"Thank you, John," he wrote. "You have helped me so much in the past. I am sure you will continue to do so—*because you are my son*. Affectionately, Max."

I carried my biological father's name, but he never chose to call me *son*. Uncle Max did that. And even as he told me he was dying, he chose to give me his blessing. With those words, in some incredible way, I was an emotional orphan no more. I was a chosen son. And I knew it because Uncle Max had made the choice to write out his blessing to me.

That is the choice I would like you to make as well.

What Do I Say?

Keep in mind that there is no wrong way to craft a blessing, and there are lots of creative right ways. And whether it comes out all at once in a rush of words or takes you a few tries and several evenings to outline and polish what you want to say, your child will cherish both what you write and what it represents about your relationship.

How you actually do the writing depends on what you are comfortable with. Some people work best in pencil on a yellow legal pad. Others can't even think without a word processor. You could even talk into a voice recorder and then transcribe your words.

Do you have more questions about composing your blessing? Check out the "Frequently Asked Questions" section on TheBlessing.com. If that doesn't answer your question, be sure and write us—you will find contact information on the site as well. Who knows? Your question may even become our featured Question of the Week.

And what should you say? Your words can be plain or poetic. They just need to carry with them a picture of your blessing that can help your child know that he or she is of high value to you. Here are a couple of examples to inspire you:

A Poetic Blessing

If you lean toward the creative or romantic side, then perhaps you can draw inspiration from this letter of blessing below. It was written by a father to his young daughter and given to her on June 11, 1948, when she was twelve years old. Today, more than fifty years later, it is still very much worth reading. I'll share the letter first; then I'll tell you who wrote it:

Dearest Joanne,

Those beautiful quaking aspens that you've seen in the forest as we have driven along have one purpose in life.

I would like to tell you about them because they remind me a lot of Mommy and you kids and me.

Those aspens are born and grown just to protect the spruce tree when it's born. As the spruce tree grows bigger and bigger the aspens gradually grow old and tired and they even die after while. But the spruce, which has had its tender self protected in its childhood, grows into one of the forest's most wonderful trees.

Now think about Mommy and me as aspens standing there quaking ourselves in the winds that blow, catching the cold snows of life, bearing the hot rays of the sun, all to protect you from those things until you are strong enough and wise enough to do them yourself. We aren't quaking from fear, but from the joy of being able to see your life develop and grow into tall straight men and women.

Just like the spruce, you have almost reached the point where you don't need us as much as you used to. Now you stand, like the young spruce, a pretty, straight young thing whose head is beginning to peep above the protection of Mommy and Daddy's watchfulness. . . .

I am telling you all this because from now on a lot of what you eventually become—a lovely woman, a happy woman and a brilliant, popular woman—depends on you.

You can't go through life being these things and at the same time frowning. You can't achieve these things and be grumpy. You have to grow so that your every deed and look reflect the glory that is now in your heart and soul.

Smile. Think right. Believe in God and His worldwide forest of men and women.

It's up to you.

I love you,
Daddy[1]

That's quite a letter, isn't it? In fact, in reflecting on it, his daughter Joanne states, "I still cry every time I read it. He was a master with words. He was a romantic."

And who was Joanne's father? He wasn't a poet, pastor, or teacher. He was a *politician*—Barry Goldwater. In fact, he is usually named as among the most hard-nosed of politicians. When he ran for president in the 1960s, he was demonized and said to be heartless. But that is not the side his daughter saw.

My point here isn't political. It is deeply personal. It's about the words that Goldwater wrote to his young daughter at a turning point in her life. I'm not saying Goldwater knew about the five elements of the blessing as he wrote them—but reread it and just look at how many elements are there.

He pictures for her a positive future. He praises his daughter in words that demonstrate a genuine commitment. He attaches high value to her even during a difficult period in her life. (For most of us, keeping a good attitude during adolescence is tough.) With the exception of meaningful touch—which is hard to provide in a letter if he didn't hand it to her or sit next to her while she read it—that letter includes every element of the biblical blessing. No wonder it still means so much to her.

So feel free, in writing your blessing for your child, to be poetic like that hard-nosed politician. But don't worry if you are more the practical, straightforward sort. You don't have to be a poet to give a meaningful blessing—as another letter shows us.

Practical Words of Praise

"Dear Michael," writes an engineer who thought long and hard before writing out a much more practical but just as precious letter to his newborn son:

As I sit beside you, and read you this letter today, I hope you'll know how much time and thought I've put into each word. After all, it's been nine long months, one week, and two days since we found out you were coming! I want you to know, today and always, that we prayed for you before you were born. That every day you were in Mommy's tummy, we prayed for you. And I want you to know that on this day when they handed you to me, the day of your birth, I had tears in my eyes and had to sit down, I was so filled with joy. We are so grateful to God for you, and so committed to being the best parents we can for you and God. This letter is the first official "birthday blessing" letter that I'm committed to writing you. Each year, as God gives me strength and life, I'll write more about why I love you, why you're so special to me, and why I'm so glad and honored to be your dad.

Your Dad[2]

You would think there wouldn't be very many words to bless a child only a few hours old, but that letter says so much so well. And so will your letter to your child. Whether your child is twelve years or twelve hours, whether your blessing is handwritten or typed out, whether you can write elegant prose or can barely spell—none of that matters. It's the words that count, and the time is now!

SHARING YOUR BLESSING
WITH YOUR CHILD

Once you have written your words of blessing, we encourage you to talk with your spouse (if you're married) and pick a special time and place to share these words with your child. If at all possible, do it face-to-face. Pick a meaningful time, place, or event—a family affair with lots of friends and relatives, a milestone celebration such as a birth or graduation, or a quiet dinner with just the two of you. Just make sure that it is at a time and place that allows you to be quiet long enough to read or recite the blessing you have written to your son or daughter.

Don't forget to include the element of meaningful, appropriate touch along with your blessing—a hand on the head, an arm around the shoulder, and hopefully a big hug. You might even want to snap a picture of the two of you together or give the child a keepsake copy of your blessing done in a special font, calligraphy, or just your best handwriting.

What if you can't be physically present—if you are deployed overseas, for instance, or divorced and living across the country? If you will be together soon, why not write out your blessing now and wait until you are together to deliver it? But don't wait too long. You can always write out your blessing in your best handwriting or format it on the computer and put it in the mail. You could even do a video of your blessing and e-mail it to your child or do the whole thing via Skype.

Keep in mind that there is no wrong way of giving a child your blessing. Even if you choose to do a special dinner and burn the hamburgers, if it rains on the one night you have counted on a starlit sky, if the dog decides to throw up just before the special event or the camera batteries fail, it doesn't really matter. If you will write down your words and make your plans, I believe you will find that God just works it out!

The fact that your child receives your blessing is far more important than any challenges you face in delivering it. It is your blessing, prepared just for him or her. And however you choose to deliver it, make sure your child has a copy of your written words. Perhaps he or she will keep it and carry it along to college or out into the world. Perhaps one day it will be tucked into a backpack as well.

 At TheBlessing.com you will find examples of a number of fun, practical, and even outrageous ways in which people have written out and shared their blessing. (We haven't had an underwater blessing letter reading yet—but I'm sure that's coming!)

DON'T LEAVE THE BLESSING TO CHANCE

Before you actually get to work on your written blessing, there are a few more things I would urge you to keep in mind. First, don't assume your children will automatically know your heart or "just figure out" what you think about them. *How* you choose to bless a child is not nearly as important as making that choice—being intentional about the blessing.

As I have shared throughout this book, my mother gave me all five of the elements of the blessing time and time again. But one very special blessing from her was almost thrown away.

After Mom passed away, my brothers and I were going through her things, trying to sort out what to keep and what to give away. This was very hard for me because I wanted to keep everything. The blue sweater she loved to wear. The little stick she held in her arthritic hands to poke the television channels on the remote (and whack the TV occasionally if someone was sharing an opinion she didn't like). Everything had a meaning and value.

But what almost got thrown out was a small notebook with a scuffed-up cover that we thought was empty. It wasn't. I picked it out of the trash bin at the last minute before it was bagged up and found this on the first page: "A Journal of Rededication to Jesus Christ."

None of us boys had ever seen this journal. Written in my mother's hand, it recorded her thoughts and prayers, dreams and hopes. I would like to share with you the last journal entry before her death. (All spelling, capitals, and quotation marks are as she wrote them.)

God has granted me yet another new beginning. There have been so many before. My hopes and dreams have been so high . . . but each time I fail. I call another driver STUPID. I make a cutting remark about another. I bring into a place of beauty discordant behavior, and thus foul up again.

But God has poured out blessing on me from the day of my birth. He has allowed me to live, "all the days of my life," at a time of great wonder, and in a State that dazzles the eyes and soul with beauty.

He has brought me a Teacher of his word who is exceptional. He has provided me with an annotated Bible, and so often restored my health.

All these plus 3 miracles of creation who are my sons.

How blessed could one woman be?

Thank you, Lord. How inadequate is language to praise you.

It is painful to me to realize those words were a moment away from being thrown out. How tragic if God hadn't stopped me and allowed me to rescue them from the trash. And how tragic if we keep our words to ourselves, assuming our kids will just somehow "know" that they have our blessing without our written or spoken words to tell them.

ACCIDENTALLY ON PURPOSE

My wife's father, George, was a hardworking, hard-drinking man, a B-17 bomber pilot in World War II. Raised on a dairy farm in Wisconsin, he did his pilot training at Arizona's Luke Air Force Base in December, and he swore that if he survived the war, he would come back there to live, where he could wear shorts in the winter.

He did just that. After the war he jumped into construction work in Arizona, got married, and fathered my Cindy. Unfortunately, he started jumping into a bottle as well, and he was an angry drunk. He was also openly hostile against any form of faith—he used to say that the nuns in his Catholic school had "beat all the religion out of" him as a child. When Cindy, his only daughter, was growing up, no one was even allowed to mention Jesus—unless, of course, you wanted to make fun of believers.

Then Cindy came to know Christ, and she began talking to her father about Jesus. He loved to debate and argue, and as a new Christian, Cindy would often get stumped by his questions. But instead of getting angry, she used her inability to respond as motivation to dig deeper into God's Word and find answers for him.

Year after year Cindy kept loving, encouraging, praying for, and otherwise blessing her father, even when he was an angry alcoholic. A turning point came when he faced a drunk-driving conviction. The judge gave him a choice between jail and AA. He chose AA, got into recovery, and mellowed . . . some.

Amazingly, incredibly, George would place his faith in Jesus a year before he passed away. His decision, a direct result of Cindy's prayers and persistence over the years, was certainly a blessing to our family. But it was an accidental meeting that happened a dozen years before he came to faith that blessed Cindy most dramatically . . . and still does today.

It was Christmastime, and we were all at a party at the home of my older brother, Joe. Joe had one of those long, narrow galley-style kitchens, barely wide enough for two people to walk through side by side. That's why my father-in-law didn't realize he was blocking Cindy's path.

Cindy was helping get platters of food out of the kitchen and onto the serving table in the other room when she walked up behind her father. He was in the middle of an animated conversation with one of our family friends and had no idea Cindy was standing behind him. And he was talking about *her*, using words she had never heard him use.

Cindy knew her father loved her. But she hadn't heard those words.

She knew her father was proud of her. But she hadn't heard those words either. Not out loud. Not directly.

Now she found herself standing behind her father, a plate of food still in her hands, listening as he went on and on about how proud he was of her. How she was the only one in his whole family (at that point) to graduate from college. What a great teacher she was and what a tremendous mother and wife she was and how she delighted him in so many ways.

Cindy just stood there in shock, listening to her father's words. Words of affirmation and praise and high value that he had never shared with her personally, he was now rattling off to a stranger. And perhaps it was that stranger's look that finally caused him to stop, look behind him, and see Cindy.

I walked into the kitchen at that exact moment—to see a father and daughter hugging each other, crying (yes, even the bomber pilot), and telling each other that they loved each other. Those were words that Cindy had waited for all her life, words she may never have heard had it not happened acciden-tally. And that is one huge reason why we encourage people to "accidentally on purpose" write out a blessing to share with their child.

A Lifetime of Blessing

Don't wait! Don't leave your blessing to chance! Make an inten-tional plan to give your son, your daughter—everyone you care about—your blessing. Write it down. Speak the words. Make a memory now and give a keepsake for tomorrow.

But don't stop there.

The kind of planned, formal blessing we have described in this chapter can be wonderful and life-changing, but if you really want your child to thrive, you will not only *give* the blessing but also *live* it, seeking out ways to include meaning-ful touch, spoken and written words, messages of high value and a special future, and evidence of active commitment in every day you spend together, every moment.

At the breakfast table and over bedtime prayers, some parents memorize a little blessing to say or sing to their chil-dren at these moments.

In the car on the way to school (that can be the perfect time for an offhand conversation with a teen).

While on the soccer field, in the movie theater, at church, at the park, or in the backyard, look for ways to inject little words of blessing in everyday conversation.

Make it a habit, and the blessings will flow through your life—as the pictures in the next chapter show.

[SIXTEEN]

Next Steps:
Five Pictures That Point the Way

IN THE PREVIOUS chapter, I urged you to take your first step on the blessing path by writing out your words of blessing and choosing a special time to share it with your child. That is a great first step. But the blessing doesn't have to be just a one-time occasion. In fact, it is something we should live out every day of our lives.

In this chapter, then, I would like to talk about the next steps you can take down the blessing path. In particular, I look at some practical ways whereby you can make the blessing a part of your everyday life with your child and with others God places in your life.

You know well by now the five elements of the blessing.

- Meaningful touch
- A spoken message
- Attaching high value

- Picturing a special future
- An active commitment

Watch how often all five show up in the following biblical pictures of Jesus—and of people who, like him, chose to look for ways to share the blessing. Each snapshot presents a vivid illustration of how we, too, can live the blessing every day of our lives.

The Washing of the Disciples' Feet

This picture is mounted in the book of John, chapter 13.

The scene is the Upper Room on the night of his arrest. Jesus is celebrating a last meal with his disciples. The table is set. The food is prepared. But before they start eating, he pulls out a basin and towel and—much to his disciples' surprise—washes their feet. They look at each other in confusion. It's a servant's job to greet guests at the door, take off their sandals, and wash the dirt from their feet. Why in the world is Jesus doing that?

"The Son of Man did not come to be served, but to serve," Jesus had said earlier in his ministry (Matt. 20:28). This is one of the pictures that show us he meant what he said.

To think that Jesus would do that for me! That he would stop to serve me, to cleanse and refresh me, to make me feel like a guest in his presence. What a picture of blessing—and it's a picture for all of us. Even if we have always been treated like the outcast or the uninvited or the tagalong, he sees us as an honored guest. And he stoops to serve us.

If you're counting, I think this picture features all five elements at once. Spoken or written words, attaching high value, picturing a special future, genuine commitment—and in this case even meaningful touch.

A similar picture comes to mind when I think about my mom, who blessed me with so many Christlike pictures over my life. I think of all the amazing ways she made us feel so valuable when we were around her. Though broken with arthritis, she was able to lift us up in so many ways . . . like diving for quarters.

We didn't have much money in our single-parent home, so our house was one of the few in our area that didn't have a pool. But there was a public pool at Perry Park down the road. On many blazing summer afternoons my mother would pull into the driveway after work and honk the horn. We would cheer as she announced we were going to the pool.

Mom never got in the water. Her arthritic knees were so bad, and pools back then weren't handicapped-friendly. But she knew how hot we were, so she would drive us to the pool, sit in all that heat on the (not-so-very) cool deck, and toss in quarters for us to dive down and catch or pick up off the bottom.

Every time we broke the surface with our fists raised high in triumph and the quarter in our hands, Mom's eyes would be shining, her twisted hands doing a soft clap. In Proverbs, remember, we are told, "Bright eyes make the heart glad." My mother was always looking for ways she could serve us kids and lift us up, both at the same time. She did it with her heart, with her eyes, and with all five elements of the blessing.

When I think of my mom, I think of one way to live the blessing . . . with a servant's heart.

 This chapter looks at five pictures of Jesus, who knew how to live out the blessing, and five pictures of how we, too, when we walk with him, can find ways of living out the blessing that will change the lives of others around us each day. It is a choice I hope you will continue to make. And at TheBlessing.com, you will find more next-step encouragement to do just that.

THE WOMAN AT THE WELL

The picture of Jesus with the woman at the well is found in John 4. We looked at this passage in chapter 4, but let's revisit it now with to see what it can tell us about living the blessing.

If you'll remember, this particular woman came to the well to draw water at noon, the hottest hour of the day. That fact alone whispers something of her reputation. Most women would have come early in the morning or at dusk when it was cool. But this woman has had five husbands, and she's not married to the man she's living with now. She probably comes at midday to avoid the gossip, the stares, the fingers pointed in her direction. And she is surprised to see a stranger there. A Jewish stranger in a Samaritan town. Jesus.

He asks for a drink, and that really throws her. "How is it that you being a Jew, ask me for a drink since I am a Samaritan woman?" It strikes her as odd not only because he is a Jew and the Jews had no dealings with the Samaritans, but also because he is a man, and men in her culture had little social contact with women. Yet to her and to her alone, Jesus gives one of the greatest revelations in all of Scripture, that "God is Spirit, and those who worship Him must worship in spirit and truth" (John 4:24).

The short conversation they have together at that well changes that woman's life. It blesses her to know that someone like Jesus would talk with someone of her reputation. And if you read the account in John, you see they have a *real* conversation. Not a monologue but a dialogue. Not a sermon but genuine interaction.

Jesus showing up in that woman's world, talking with her about her life, and respecting her dignity—that's a truly beautiful picture of the way God comes to each of us. Meeting us where we are. Engaging us in conversation. Treating us with respect. Moving us closer and closer to him.

And here, again, we can count the blessing elements pictured in that scene. Not meaningful touch, which would be inappropriate in that cultural context. But Jesus' words surely touched something deep within the Samaritan woman. Talk about picturing a special future for and attaching high value to a person. And the offer of living water—could there be a more perfect picture of active commitment?

I'm glad that I've had people show up in my life that way. I have already mentioned Doug Barram, my high school Young Life leader. He was an adult, yet he entered my high school world, meeting me on the football field or at the gym, talking with me about my life, treating me like a real person, not just a kid, moving me closer and closer to the well of living water.

I remember one time in particular. It was my senior year. Doug picked up seven of us who were in his Bible study—all seniors, each of whom he had led to Christ—and took us out to breakfast. He wanted to get us all together before we left for college. After we finished eating, he had each of us say what our goals and dreams were.

My brother, Jeff, said he wanted to be a doctor, which he now is. One of the other guys wanted to be a commercial pilot. One by one we told each other our dreams. When my turn came, I said I wanted to get my doctorate, write books, and help people.

Every one of my friends at the table laughed when I said that. They knew I was a terrible student. I had gotten into college on academic probation, and I would get into seminary and my doctoral program the same way. So everyone had good reason to laugh.

But two people at that table didn't laugh—my brother, who has always been wonderfully supportive and sought to give me his blessing, and Doug. He took me seriously even while the others at the table were roaring with laughter. He quieted them down and then shared with them what he saw in me, including the ability to do everything I had said I wanted to do.

They smirked and moved on, but I have never forgotten that picture of an adult meeting with a bunch of high school kids around a table, engaging us in a dialogue about our lives, treating us all with such respect.

Giving me the blessing.

That's another way we can live out the blessing day by day—by affirming goals and dreams and seeing the potential in someone's life.

The Commissioning of Peter

Here is yet another picture . . . this one found in Matthew 16.

Jesus takes this brash and impulsive fisherman, asks him one question, and on the basis of his answer, commissions him to lead his church.

It was not what Jesus *heard* from Peter that inspired his choice but what he *saw* in Peter—his potential. Others saw only the sharp and abrasive edges; Jesus saw a foundation stone. While others saw unpredictability, Jesus saw stability. Others saw the rough hands of a fisherman, Jesus saw hands that would hold the keys of the kingdom of heaven. He saw Peter not for who he was but for who he was to become.

What a picture that Peter was blessed with in that moment. What a picture we all are blessed with when we are told that we have been predestined to be conformed to the image of Christ

(Rom. 8:29), that he who has begun a good work in us will bring it to completion (Phil. 1:6). What potential for a special future he sees in us.

I was blessed with a picture of a special future that, again, came from my mom. It happened when my twin brother, Jeff, the A student, brought home his senior term paper. He had made an A-plus this time, and Mom was appropriately proud.

But I had done a term paper too. Of course, I hadn't started it until the night before it was due . . . and I had lost the instructions about doing the footnotes correctly . . . and I had even run out of typewriter ribbon (remember those?) and had to write the last two pages by hand. Those were details. I was interested in the content, the ideas, and I believed that what I had written was nothing short of outstanding. But my teacher went with the details, and I carried home a D-plus that day. I slowly handed over my paper and waited with my head down as she read every word—including the negative comments that bathed the paper in red ink.

"You could have woken me up," she said gently. "I would have taken you to get more typewriter ribbon."

"I know, Mom," I said and waited for the rest of the lecture on how far I was falling behind. Instead, she moved me forward by light-years with her words of blessing.

"John, look at me."

Mom was always good at making you look her in the eye when she talked to you—when she told you something important. What she told me was the last thing I thought I would ever hear from her (a former A-plus student herself).

"Forget the details," she said. "You do such a good job of using words when you write—I wouldn't be surprised if God used your words someday to help others."

Can you imagine? *Me?* I had been kicked out of fifth grade. I was barely passing most of my courses. None of my teachers were predicting a special future for me. Yet my mother's words of blessing, her depiction of a special future, were so important to me in that moment—so encouraging, so hope filled, so much like Jesus.

Living the blessing means looking for ways to discern potential and affirm it—and we change lives when we make the effort to do that.

THE HEMORRHAGING WOMAN

This picture is one of my favorites. You can find it framed in Luke 8.

Jesus is on his way to heal a dying twelve-year-old girl, the daughter of a synagogue official named Jairus. As he walks, the crowd presses in around him. So the scene is fairly intense. A girl's life is at stake. People jostle and reach for him. And into this scene a chronically ill woman, someone who has been plagued with constant bleeding for many years, pushes through the crowd. She is thinking to herself, *If I can just get close enough to touch his garment, that will be enough.*

Finally she gets close enough and touches the fringe of his garment. Barely a tug, but he feels it. And he stops. He calls to her and she comes, trembling, to fall down before him. And ever so tenderly he tells her, "Daughter . . . your faith has made you well. Go in peace."

That is one of my favorite biblical scenes because it shows me how sensitive Jesus is to the slightest bit of faith we can extend to him. We don't have to have the right words or the right timing or the right anything. All we have to do is reach out to him, and he will stop for us.

I also love that story because it reminds me of one last picture of my mom. Lots of pictures of my mom, actually. During my senior year in high school, Jeff and I had a ritual we enjoyed with several of our friends. After we dropped off our Saturday night dates (if we even had a date), we would meet at a Jack-in-the-Box restaurant at eleven and wolf down an entire menu of tacos, burgers, fries, and shakes.

Then around midnight Jeff and I would head home for another ritual. We would walk down the hall to Mom's room and touch her lightly in the dark to see if she was awake. Then we'd flop down on either side of her and talk about our evening, our dates if we'd had them, the movie we had seen, and the people we had met. The conversation would drift to what our week had been like, what had gone well, what hadn't. We'd share our dreams and tell each other the details of our lives, all there in the dark on our mom's bed.

Then one Saturday night, after months of this ritual, a thought struck me.

"Mom?" I asked. "Does it bother you, us waking you up so late to talk?"

"Boys," she said, patting us in the dark. "I can *always* go back to sleep. But I won't always have you boys here to talk to. Wake me up anytime."

I knew she meant it. She was so sensitive to the touch of her boys who came in at midnight. Even when she was asleep. Even when she had to get up early the next day. She was never so tired or so pressured that she couldn't feel that touch in the dark. She always had time to look for ways to bless us. *Always.*

And that is yet another illustration of what it means to live the blessing. It means being sensitive and aware of the needs of others—and being willing to stop what we are doing to minister to those needs.

The Picture of Our Heavenly Father

This picture is tucked away in Luke 15, and it's a familiar one.

Jesus presented it to show the Pharisees the joy there is in heaven when just one wayward person turns around and comes home to the Father's arms.

You remember how it goes. The prodigal son decides he wants to see the world and sow some wild oats along the way. But when the money from his inheritance runs out, he finds himself destitute in a distant land, and the only job he can find is in a pigsty.

What brings him to his senses and puts him on the road back is the memory of his father's generosity: "How many of my father's hired servants have bread enough and to spare, and I perish with hunger!" (Luke 15:17). So he makes his way home, and his father spots him. Look at how he responds:

> When he was still a great way off, his father saw him and had compassion, and ran and fell on his neck and kissed him. And the son said to him, "Father, I have sinned against heaven and in your sight, and am no longer worthy to be called your son."
>
> But the father said to his servants, "Bring out the best robe and put it on him, and put a ring on his hand and sandals on his feet. And bring the fatted calf here and kill it, and let us eat and be merry; for this my son was dead and is alive again; he was lost and is found." And they began to be merry. (vv. 20–24)

It's all there in that one picture. The eyes that searched for him. The heart that went out to him. The legs that ran to him. The arms that embraced him. The lips that kissed him. It's all there, and it's all for us—for you and for me and for all of us who never received a blessing from our father (or mother). Never experienced the attention or the understanding. Never knew the compassion, the embraces, the forgiveness, the restoration, the love, the joy, the delight a loving parent shares with a beloved child. Never knew the patient commitment of a parent who is in it for the long haul.

Someone once said that a child is not likely to find a father in God unless he finds something of God in his father. I never found that in my biological father. But I did find it in my spiritual father, Doug Barram. And finding something of God in that father made it easier to find a father in God.

The first Bible verse Doug gave me to memorize was Hebrews 13:5. I memorized it from the J. B. Phillips translation: "God has said, I will never leave you nor forsake you."

I will never forget that verse or the impact it first had on me. God said he *would not* fail me, *would not* forsake me. Under no circumstances would he pack his bags and walk out of my life. He was going to stay, and he was going to stay *forever*.

Could there be a father like that in all the universe?

[SEVENTEEN]

Last Words:
Living the Blessing for a Lifetime

A FEW YEARS ago my wife, Cindy, and I were teaching about the blessing at a conference for physicians and their spouses. That's when we met little Aaron's mother. She came up quietly. She shared her story softly. Yet it left a profound impact on our lives—that is, after Cindy and I had stopped crying and thanking God for what we had heard.

It seems that several years before, this woman and her husband (both physicians, by the way) had traveled from out of state to attend a similar conference of ours. They left their precious three-year-old son, Aaron, at home with a babysitter. While they were gone, Aaron began to spike a fever. The babysitter called, then called again. But the cell phone reception wasn't great in the hall, and it took them some time before they could return her call. By the time they did talk, the sitter was terribly worried about their son, particularly because his fever was so high.

Imagine two doctors, thousands of miles from their hurting

son, unable to do anything to help. Needless to say, they left for home immediately, but by the time they got there, little Aaron had been diagnosed with viral meningitis and sustained profound hearing loss as a result of the fever.

The parents, of course, were devastated when they got this news. But they determined their son's hearing loss wouldn't stop them from blessing him—not for a single day.

LIVING THE BLESSING

A Blessing Prayer

Lord, may our children never have to search for words or be left wondering if they are of value to us or to you. Help us to bless them, Lord—with our words, with our actions, with our whole lives. Remind us not to leave our words to chance but to choose to bless our sons or daughters all the days of our lives. In the name of Jesus, from whom all blessings flow, amen.

Up until the day their son lost his hearing, this couple had done something they had seen on one of our videos. The video showed Cindy and me singing a simple little blessing song we had made up for Kari and Laura when they were little. We used it to wake up the kids with a blessing in the morning. We would hug them and sing,

Good morning, good morning, how are you today?
The Lord bless you and keep you throughout the day.
We love you, we love you, we love you, Kari (or Laura).

Aaron's mom and dad had thought our song was cute and adopted it as a way to bless their son in the mornings. Ever since he was tiny, they had been singing, "We love you, we love you, we love you, Aaron."

But now Aaron couldn't hear that good-morning song or their blessing. So they immediately set out to learn the words in sign language. That way, as Aaron grew older, he wouldn't miss a day of hearing that he was special and valuable to them, that God had a special future for him, and that his parents would always be committed to him.

I think of all the children I have met whose parents never bothered to say "I love you" even once to them. Who never told them anything about their future except words like, "Don't take algebra. That's for the smart kids." Who would never take the time to write a blessing letter, no matter how much it could mean to their child.

And then I hear stories like Aaron's—stories about parents who are going to give the blessing to their child no matter what the challenge. And I am praying that one million parents like Aaron's will step up to the plate and hit it out of the park by passing on the blessing to their own child . . . and many others.

And may a million lives be changed in the process.

 Thank you so much for taking this journey with us and many blessings to you as you go about living the blessing in your family. Please go to TheBlessing.com/Chapter 17 for a final video message from Dr. Trent.

Afterword

An Invitation to Take the Blessing Challenge

REMEMBER THE BLESSING Challenge initiative we talked about at the beginning of this book? We are looking to involve a million parents and a thousand churches in this new campaign to bring the blessing to a new generation—and we would love for you to be a part.

How do you join? If you are a parent, just go to TheBlessing. com and click on "Take the Blessing Challenge." If you are a pastor or a church leader, we would like you to consider something else.

We are calling for a thousand churches nationwide to pick either Mother's Day, Father's Day, or any one Sunday in August 2011 for a special message on the blessing that encourages and builds up families and calls them to the Blessing Challenge. We will provide starter kits, including sample sermon outlines and power point slides. The key is simply to teach and preach on the blessing, then point people to a link on your church website that takes them to The Blessing

Challenge. For churches and pastors wanting more tools or encouragement to help others live out the blessing, we offer small group studies and certificates and for credit courses on the blessing at www.TheBlessing.com. Dr. Tony Wheeler and I also conduct seminars for churches: The Blessing Challenge for Parents, The Blessing Challenge for Marriage, and The Blessing Challenge for Emerging Adults.

From sermon outlines to small group materials, from consulting and strategy for building a faith-at-home driven ministry that helps families live out the blessing to pointing churches to our amazing HomePointe/StrongFamilies Centers, we stand ready to help churches across the country and beyond (see www.drivefaithhome.com for an on-campus way of building the blessing into your church).

Remember, you don't have to take the Blessing Challenge in order to give the blessing. But we hope you will. You'll become part of a huge blessing community, a million parents in a thousand churches who are committed to making the blessing an intentional part of their lives.

Appendix

Become a Blessing Champion

Perhaps this is your first time reading *The Blessing*. Or maybe, like me, you read the book twenty-five years ago when it was first released. Every chapter seemed to awaken in me a sense of hope that I was not fated to replicate the lifestyle choices my mom and dad had made.

When I was seven years old, my father divorced my mother and moved to another state. I moved to Greenleaf, Idaho, with my mom and younger brother to live near my grandparents who helped Mom raise the two of us. I played basketball and football in high school, so I had some great Christian coaches in my life. I attended youth group at my church and went to a Christian high school. All of these things were helpful, but they didn't fill my need to be blessed by my absentee father, and they didn't stop the awareness within me that something was missing.

When I was eighteen, I moved to Haviland, Kansas, to attend Friends Bible College (now called Barclay College). And it was during those college years, while I was doing everything I could to find a sense of internal security and hope for my future, that I had an encounter that changed my life.

It happened during my junior year. I was on the basketball

team, and we had an away game at another college. The plan was to stay there overnight before heading home the next day. But after the game I found myself wide awake and unable to sleep. My buddy and I didn't like the old, dirty dorm rooms we had been given as our accommodations for the night by the team we had just trounced on the court. We went on a hunt for better accommodations and came upon a room that better fit our tastes—a nicely appointed space with two beautiful leather couches. Too young and bold to be deterred by the sign on the door that read "President's Office," we immediately decided to spend the night right there.

On the coffee table in front of my "bed" for the night, I found a book and a magazine. The magazine was called *Family in Focus* (published by Focus on the Family). And the book was a little volume called—you guessed it—*The Blessing*.

That night I finally had a clear picture of what it looked like to love a wife and bless her as God intended. I became excited about being a father someday. Like so many adult children of divorce, I had been fearful of whether I could really do a good job of loving and being there for my family. That may sound like a lot of internal changes taking place, all because of reading a single book, but I believe God used that night to radically change my life. I saw and embraced a biblical model of healthy relating that would become my life goal and a message I knew others simply must know.

A few months later God brought an amazing woman named Stacey into my life. We eventually got married (just celebrated our twenty-third wedding anniversary), had three amazing children, and have tried to live out the five elements of the blessing as a couple and as a family.

After completing a master's degree in family therapy at Friends University and a PhD in family life education and consultation from Kansas State University, I became a marriage and family therapist. I also pastored churches and spoke as often as I could on my favorite topic—helping marriages and families to be strong and living out John Trent's message of the blessing.

Then in 1997, Stacey and I moved to Arizona to plant a church. Advised that a good way to meet new people was to get a job that put us in contact with the community, I was behind the counter waiting on Starbuck customers one day when I looked up to see a familiar face. "You're John Trent!" I said. I recognized him from the photo on the back of the book, and I had seen him at a distance when he spoke at a Promise Keepers I had once attended.

When I was able to take a break, I shared my story with him, how *The Blessing* had changed my family and the direction of my ministry. The friendship we established then lasted long after I quit working at that Starbucks. Over the next few years we became very close friends. I even began working with Dr. Trent and his StrongFamilies.com ministry, speaking about the blessing message wherever I was invited.

Then in June of 2009, my family and I moved back to Haviland, Kansas, where I teach at the same school where I first read *The Blessing*. In addition to teaching I also had the honor of helping launch and becoming the executive director and vice president of the Dr. John Trent Institute for the Blessing at Barclay College. Talk about the Lord going full circle in a way I couldn't have imagined!

What Does the Institute for the Blessing Do?

Our primary objective is to help individuals go deeper in understanding this life-changing, life-giving concept called *the blessing.* Our specific goal for the next fifteen years is to help train people to become *blessing champions.* We do this in a number of ways:

- We offer webinars and online certificate courses on living the blessing that help individuals "reverse the curse" and deal with past hurts.
- We team with churches to train and equip church leaders. Along with Kurt Bruner (part of our StrongFamilies.com team and pastor of spiritual formation at LakePointe Church in Rockwall, Texas), we have also begun helping churches set up HomePointe/ StrongFamilies/Blessing Centers that help moms and dads drive faith home.
- We partner with national ministries such as Focus on the Family and with several key publishers such as Thomas Nelson to promote a blessing lifestyle.
- And we align with Barclay College to offer certificate of completion courses, undergraduate and graduate programs, and—Lord willing—soon we'll even have a doctoral program in transformational leadership.

Dr. Trent and I would be honored if you'd consider going deeper in living out the blessing by taking part in a course, scheduling a seminar, or just joining with us in making sure that this biblical message impacts a whole new generation of parents. Just go to our website at www.TheBlessing.com and click on the Institute for the Blessing button. May God richly bless you as you seek Him and seek to bless others!

— Dr. Tony Wheeler,
Executive Director and Vice President
The Institute for the Blessing at Barclay College

Notes

Chapter 1: To Change a Life

1. See Mark 9:37, where Jesus, in discussing true greatness with his disciples, picks up a little one in his arms and says, "Whoever receives one child like this . . . receives Me" (NASB). As laudable as it is to want to "help the children," doing something great begins with that "one child" within your reach.

2. These five elements of the blessing are incredibly powerful, even if you are reading this as a deployed service man or woman or are a noncustodial parent living in a different city or state from your child.

3. Not all studies on transferring faith to our children are as draconian as Barna's research; however, his are sobering thoughts for those of us serious about passing on our faith to our children. See George Barna, *Transforming Children into Spiritual Champions* (Ventura, CA: Regal Books, 2003), 33–34.

4. Dr. Tony Wheeler, who serves as executive director at the Institute for the Blessing at Barclay College as well as heads up our upcoming Blessing Institute Focus on the Family campus, offers an audio message on this topic that I think is essential listening for any loving parent, spouse, or friend. To download this message, visit TheBlessing.com and look in our "Audio CD and Downloadable Resources" section. In late 2011, this message is set to come out in a book and workbook for small groups. Visit the bookstore at TheBlessing.com to find out more about upcoming resources on giving and living the blessing.

Chapter 4: A Life-and-Death Choice

1. Brown, Driver, and Briggs, *A Hebrew and English Lexicon of the Old Testament* (Oxford: Clarendon Press, 1974), 311, vb. "live." See along with James Strong, *Strong's Exhaustive Concordance of the Bible* (Hendrickson Publishers), citation 2416. The word *life* carries definitions such as "to be quickened," "running," "springing," and to "troop." We are "alive" when we are animated to "get moving" and, like a "troop" of soldiers, move or step towards an objective.

2. Death, "to depart, to remove, to step away," Brown, Driver, and Briggs, *Hebrew and English Lexicon*, 559. The New Testament word for death, *thanatos*, also carries this idea of stepping away.

3. Brown, Driver, and Briggs, *Hebrew and English Lexicon*, 139.

4. Honor, "to be heavy, weighty, honored," Brown, Driver, and Briggs, *Hebrew and English Lexicon*, 457. The idea of coins in a scale can even be seen in one way this word is translated as an "offering."

5. Curse, "to be slight, of water, be abated," Brown, Driver, and Briggs, *Hebrew and English Lexicon*, 886b. To see a picture of this in scripture, go to Genesis 8:3, where the flood waters are "cursed," literally meaning, "the waters abated." It is, in part, pulling away life-giving water from someone that we curse them.

Chapter 6: The First Element: Meaningful Touch

1. Robert Salt, "Affectionate Touch Between Fathers and Preadolescent Sons," *Journal of Marriage and the Family* 53 (August 1991): 545.

2. Job 41:15–17; also see Brown, Driver, and Briggs, *Hebrew and English Lexicon*, 621.

3. Salt, "Affectionate Touch," 545.

4. Ibid.

5. Ibid.

6. The blessing of Ephraim and Manasseh also had a unique spiritual message. When Jacob "crossed" his hands and blessed the younger with the older son's blessing, it was a picture of God's election.

7. Charles F. Pfeiffer, Howard F. Vos, and John Rea, eds., *Wycliffe Bible Encyclopedia* (Chicago: Moody Press, 1975), 750.

8. Harvey Richard Schiffman, *Sensation and Perception: An Integrated Approach* (New York: John Wiley & Sons, 1982), 107.

9. Frank A. Geldard, "Body English," *Psychology Today* (December 1968): 44.

10. Dolores Krieger, "Therapeutic Touch: The Imprimatur of Nursing," *American Journal of Nursing* (May 1975): 784.

11. *UCLA Monthly*, Alumni Association News, March–April 1981, 1.

12. *Reader's Digest*, January 1992, 21.

13. *Current Health* 13, no. 2 (1986): 13.

14. *Parents* 64, no. 2 (1989).

15. L. W. Linkous and R. M. Stutts, "Passive Tactile Stimulation Effects on the Muscle Tone of Hypotonic Developmentally Delayed Young Children," *Perceptual and Motor Skills* 1, no. 3 (December 1990): 951–54.

16. F. B. Dresslar, "The Psychology of Touch," *American Journal of Psychology* 6 (1984): 316.

17. Marcia Mark and Perla Werner, "Agitation and Touch in the Nursing Home," *Psychological Reports* 64, no. 3, part 2 (1989): 1020.

18. Ibid., 1023.

19. *Health* 21, no. 10 (October 1989), 73.

20. James Hardison, *Let's Touch* (New York: Prentice-Hall, 1980).

21. Helen Colton, *The Gift of Touch* (New York: Seaview/Putnam, 1983), 102.

22. *Reader's Digest*, 21.

23. Edgar Wycoff and Jill Holley, "Effects of Flight Attendant's Touch upon Airline Passenger's Perceptions of the Attendant and the Airline," *Perceptual and Motor Skills* 1, no. 3, part 1 (December 1990): 932–34.

24. Colton, *The Gift of Touch*, 49.

NOTES

25. Arthur Janov, "For Control, Cults Must Ease the Most Profound Pains," *Los Angeles Times*, 10 December 1978, part 6, 3.
26. Marc H. Hollender, "The Wish to Be Held," *Archives of General Psychiatry* 22 (1970): 445.
27. Ibid., 446.
28. Ross Campbell, *How to Really Love Your Child* (Wheaton, IL: Victor Books, 1977), 73.
29. Alfred Edersheim, *The Life and Times of Jesus the Messiah, Part Two* (Grand Rapids: Wm. B. Eerdmans Publishing Co., 1972), 329.
30. Sidney Jourand, *Psychology Today* 22, no. 3 (March 1988): 31.

Chapter 7: The Second Element: A Spoken Message

1. Gary Smalley, *The Key to Your Child's Heart* (Waco, TX: Word Books, 1984). See the chapter on "Balancing Loving Support Through Contracts," pp. 77–107.
2. Jack Burtin, "Goodbye . . . Be Good to Each Other," *USA Today*, August 19, 1985, 1.

Chapter 8: The Third Element: Attaching High Value

1. Brown, Driver, and Briggs, *Hebrew and English Lexicon*, 139.
2. That is why Psalm 95:6 translates the word *bless* as "to bow the knee" when it says, "Come let us worship the LORD and bow before Him" (literally, bless him).
3. J. D. Douglas, "Lion of Judah," *New Bible Dictionary* (Grand Rapids: Wm. B. Eerdman's Publishing, 1971 edition), 742.
4. Some circles dispute how Solomon, with all his many wives, could be a model for a godly marriage. One can see a commentary on the Song of Solomon for a fuller explanation, but in brief here are two reasons why we feel Solomon's story can still help any married couple today. First, Solomon did not begin to take foreign wives and concubines until later in life, after his visit by the queen of Sheba. Song of Solomon is dated by most scholars as being written early in his reign as king. More important, any person, including Solomon, could leave his first love when he stops walking with God. During Solomon's later years, when he took many wives, his fellowship with God was certainly not where it was when he asked for the gift of wisdom.
5. S. Craig Glickman, *A Song for Lovers* (Downers Grove, IL: InterVarsity Press, 1974), 48.

Chapter 9: The Fourth Element: Picturing a Special Future

1. M. J. Cohen, *The Jewish Celebration Book* (Philadelphia: The Jewish Publication Society of America, 1946), 108.
2. Jay Stifler, *The Epistle to the Romans* (Chicago: Moody Press, 1983), 119.
3. While we do not recommend the book because of its secular bent and conclusions, William S. Appleton's *Fathers and Daughters* (New York: Berkley Books, 1984) has a number of chilling studies that have been done on the destruction that happens when a father has a poor relationship with his daughter.
4. We would like to extend our special thanks to Dr. Jeffrey M. Trent, associate professor of medicine, University of Arizona, for putting this example into "everyday English" for us.

261

Chapter 10: The Fifth Element: An Active Commitment

1. For a helpful discussion on this point, see Charles Swindoll, *You and Your Child* (Nashville: Thomas Nelson, 1977), 27–32.
2. Gary Smalley, *The Key to Your Child's Heart* (Dallas: Word, 1984), Chapter 2, "Expressing Loving Support—The Most Important Aspect of Raising Children."
3. Dewey Roussel, "Message of the White Dove," *Reader's Digest*, September 1984, 29.

Chapter 11: Homes That Withhold the Blessing

1. For an excellent discussion of our need today for a time of "Sabbath rest," see Gordon MacDonald's *Ordering Your Private World* (Nashville: Thomas Nelson, 1984), the chapter titled "Rest Beyond Leisure."
2. Quoted by Roger Hawley, "The Family Blessing: Implications for Counseling," unpublished paper presented at the Texas Counsel of Family Relations Conference, 1983.
3. H. Norman Schwarzkopf with Peter Petre, *It Doesn't Take a Hero* (New York: Bantam Books, 1992), 19.

Chapter 12: Half-Blessed

1. Quotation by Rev. Steven Lyon in "Loving Your Children God's Way," unpublished message given in Dallas, Texas, 1983.
2. Robert Barnes, *Winning the Heart of Your Stepchild* (Grand Rapids: Zondervan, 1997). See also Ron L. Deal, *The Smart Stepfamily* (Bloomington, Minn.: Bethany House, 2006) and Ron Deal's excellent website SuccessfulStepfamilies.com.

Chapter 13: If You Missed the Blessing

1. An excellent book we recommend that deals with the impact family influences can have on both the creation and cure of substance abuse is Jeffery VanVonderen, *Good News for the Chemically Dependent* (Nashville: Thomas Nelson, 1985).
2. Richard A. McCormisk, "Affective Disorders among Pathological Gamblers Seeking Treatment," *American Journal of Psychiatry* 141, no. 2 (1984): 215.

Chapter 14: Reversing the Curse

1. See Martin Seligman, *Learned Optimism* (New York: Pocket Books, 1990).
2. Christopher Peterson and Lisa M. Bossio, *Health and Optimism* (New York: The Free Press, 1991), 81.

Chapter 15: First Steps: A Written Blessing

1. "Dad's Letter Offers Parable for Eldest daughter," AZCentral.com, June 3, 1998, http://www.azcentral.com/specials/special25/articles/0603goldwater.html.
2. A personal letter shared with me by the engineer in question.

About the Authors

JOHN TRENT, PHD, is president of Strong Families.com and founder of the Institute for the Blessing at Barclay College. John is a sought-after speaker and an award-winning author of more than twenty books, including six books for children. He has been a featured guest on numerous radio and television programs across the country and leads The Blessing Challenge, a joint partnership with Focus on the Family and StrongFamilies.com. John and his wife, Cindy, have been married for more than thirty years and have two grown daughters, Kari and Laura.

DR. GARY SMALLEY, one of the foremost experts on family relationships, has written or cowritten more than sixty books and thirty-five videos, selling more than 6 million copies. He has more than forty years of experience as a teacher and counselor. A best-selling and award-winning author, Smalley has appeared on hundreds of local and national radio and television shows, including *Oprah*, *Larry King Live*, *Fox & Friends*, and NBC's *Today*. He and his wife, Norma, have been married forty-six years and have three grown children, Kari, Greg, and Michael, all in full-time ministry.

Take the Blessing Challenge today—and help your kids thrive throughout the year!

Now, Focus on the Family can support you with daily ways to live out the Blessing Challenge for years to come, no matter where you are in the parenting stages.

FocusOnTheFamily.com/parenting
24/7 support with content and online communities for each parenting stage.

1-800-A-FAMILY (232-6459)
Speak with a family care specialist Monday–Friday, 6:00 a.m. - 8:00 p.m., MST.

Check out all the great resources from Focus on the Family for more ways to bless your child for years to come.

Thriving Family®
Get sensible, relevant, biblically-based marriage and parenting insights and guidance in a magazine! Each issue helps you learn more about loving your spouse, focusing on your child's age and stage, and passing on your faith to your children.

Focus on the Family® *Clubhouse*® and
Focus on the Family® *Clubhouse Jr.*®
Our monthly children's magazines give you numerous opportunities to connect with and bless your children. Hilarious jokes, activities and faith-building Bible stories can draw your family closer together . . . and closer to God.

Find these resources and more at: **FocusOnTheFamily.com/magazines.**

© 2011 Focus on the Family

FOCUS ON THE FAMILY®